the Dawson Slant

A sideways look at life on the Fylde Coast by the late, great Les.

Edited by Steve Singleton

A special publication brought to you by

The Gazette

Acknowledgements

Thanks chiefly go to Les Dawson's widow Tracy for her kind permission to reproduce *The Dawson Slant* weekly column from the 1980s. It is hoped this book will be a timely tribute to Les, coinciding with the unveiling of his statue in the Garden of Fame on St Annes seafront. In addition, thanks go to Gazette chief librarian Carole Davies, secretary Suzanne Steedman and Mark Borland from the photographic department.

Foreword

There's no doubt Les was a frustrated journalist at heart!

Writing was his real passion. When he was working and touring he would scribble away in his notebooks, honing his routines, filling page after page with gags and ripostes, which he developed and played with and improvised on.

When he was at home he would shut himself away in his study, and the red-hot pages would fly from his battered old typewriter – comic novels, monologues, scripts, pantomime lines, gags, whatever.

He took his writing very seriously and with thirteen books to his credit, I'm sure that if he were alive today he would spent a lot of his time writing.

Les was also particularly proud of his Northern roots; he loved his home life in Lytham and being on the doorstep of Britain's top seaside resort, Blackpool.

He always looked forward to receiving his nightly copy of *The Gazette* – and was thrilled when the newspaper agreed to publish *The Dawson Slant* in 1982.

It was a whimsical look at life and showed his love of the Fylde coast and the humour he found within it.

I would personally like to thank *The Gazette* for republishing these columns in a souvenir book and hope it brings enjoyment to old and new fans alike.

Above all I hope that the real Les comes through these pages, and that they make you laugh – as if Les was coming out for one more encore.
That would cheer him no end!

Tracy Dawson

Introduction

Prepare to laugh out loud as the late, great comedian Les Dawson takes a sideways look at life on the Fylde Coast!

Lugubrious Les adopted the Fylde as his home when stardom finally came his way. He became one of Lytham St Annes' most famous adopted sons in 1975 and an unstinting ambassador for Britain's top seaside resort, Blackpool, until his untimely death in 1993.

When encouraged to take a well-earned foreign holiday, Les once joked: "If I go abroad, I'll just get drunk on cheap plonk, baste in the sun and probably return home with the runs. I'll stick to Blackpool and Lytham St Annes. It's smashing – I love living here."

Les Dawson 1993

A blue plaque, honouring one of the world's comedy legends, was mounted by Comic Heritage outside his Ansdell home in 1995 and a £60,000 statue of Les was unveiled in a new Garden of Fame, next to St Annes Pier, in October 2008.

Lancashire's own master of mirth had such a strong belief in community that he even offered to write for his local newspaper, and The Gazette was more than delighted to snap him up!

The Dawson Slant was the name given to the comical column in which Les sprinkled his inimitable style on "parish pump" news throughout 1982 and 1983. With a serious love of writing, Les revered the comic style of S.J. Perelman and P.G. Wodehouse.

He loved the Beachcomber series from the Sunday Express, which he took as the benchmark for his Gazette column – a suitably scatterbrained series that covered all sorts of unrelated items – complete with a healthy smattering of local place names.

Our new book faithfully reproduces those weekly jottings, and together with a host of fun images of laughmaker Les from The Gazette archives, is sure to raise a smile and spark many fond memories for his friends and fans from the Fylde Coast and far beyond.

Steve Singleton
Blackpool Gazette
September 2008

the Dawson Slant

29 July 1982

At last most noble reader, this seaside broadsheet has a column worthy of the printing presses that Caxton sold them.

For the first time in history, since the Gazette was founded as a wrapper for better class chips, you will revel in the headlines behind the headlines. I want no praise for it ...no eulogy...just a fortnight's holiday in Malta will do.

The world shall now know that two of the elephants in the zoo are battery driven. I may eventually end up in a blocked culvert, but truth and the burning desire for money spur me on.

Les and Queen of the Lights Leigh Davies at the Blackpool Illuminations preview in July 1982.

A PAIR of Cromwell's socks were found in a fisherman's waistcoat last night. An expert from Sotheby's stated that they could be priceless if they still smell.

A Blackpool landlady who accidentally gave a holidaymaker an overdose of meat and veg at dinner, is still in the intensive care unit in Victoria Hospital.

The Mayor of Lytham laid a foundation stone last Tuesday and is doing as well as can be expected.

Les, Tracy and new arrival Charlotte at a rose queen crowing at Fairhaven White Church in June 1993.

Very carefully, for instance, the discovery of North Sea Vindaloo Curry has been kept away from the public. The find apparently is enormous, stretching as it does from Gateshead to Bridlington, and – already – the Indian high commissioner in Bradford has stated that if we exploit it, they will ban tins of Brown Windsor soup in New Delhi. Some experts believe that more is to be found in Fairhaven Lake, but by the time St Annes wakes up to the fact it will have clotted and gone off. The curry is easy to retrieve, all one has to do is wade out and suck it up through a length of conduit and drain fish droppings off it. It's nice with a salad and you can keep it in a hat.

———————————————

The strike at the Bispham pot gnome factory goes on. Workers are asking for a ten per cent rise and free cheese in return for putting glazed flamingos in rubber boxes. The management have refused on the grounds that clay elves were once parcelled this way and nobody got any extra for it. Miriam Cuttle, the spokeswoman for the workers, denies she stole the designs for a new fishpond pixie in moulded slate and hid the foreman's teeth as she did so, and is suing Alf Bone for threatening her with a plastic owl.

———————————————

The American draughtsman who was caught blowing omelettes through his vest in Preston, has been remanded on bail for a week. His name is Roscoe Chip and his father was a lapsed Jesuit. The policeman who arrested the American said in court that he caused great distress to a lame streaker who was brought up by a Rhode Island Red. Mr Chip also plays a mouth organ and once auditioned in a permissive launderette.

Concern among conservationists is growing over the fate of Morecambe whelks. Apparently these whelks have poor eyesight and small noses, and so cannot wear glasses which they will have to wear in order to see through the silt coming from the seabed. They are not mating as they should, and, indeed, it was reported from Grange-over-Sands, that a rampant whelk was seen trying to mount a discarded yoghurt carton. Miss Preece-Flopp, the trombone varnisher from Warton, is trying to raise money to build a clinic for middle-aged whelks in the change of life, a place – she said – where they can have their teeth scraped and watch Crossroads.

A Fleetwood clown who lost his trousers on a ferris wheel, refuses to come down. His wife has been throwing hot porridge up to him.

Age: How dare you!

Place of birth: Manchester (near mother).

Married/Single: Married.

Children: No: the wife's a grown woman (five actually!).

Occupation: Writer/ entertainer (all round good egg).

Star sign: Aquarius (but beautifully marked).

the Dawson Slant

5 August 1982

Swiss-born, Blackpool-based scientist, Dr Helmut Clack, has startled the world with a theory that braised carrots, when buried in a bucket of hot suet, become oversexed and bad tempered. Speaking to a congress of rented clairvoyants in Oldham, Dr Clack attacked the Government for not taking him seriously enough. A scuffle broke out when a left-wing snooker player threw a trowel at the good doctor who responded by standing on his head and shouting that 'Hurricane' Higgins was one of the Beverley Sisters.

———————————

Lovers of Olde Tyme Music Hall will be delighted to hear that Max Plumm is getting better after he collapsed at his home in Kirkham after cheating at Monopoly. For years he was part of a variety act called: The Masked Gurkhas and Winnie. In 1923, he danced with the Prince of Wales on the rim of a tuba at the Sandbach Braces Festival, and in September of that year, his niece and four pigs were sucked down a culvert.

———————————

There is grave concern over the mental state of the Fleetwood clown who lost his trousers on a ferris wheel. He still refuses to wear a kilt sent to him by Kenneth McKellar, and he won't come down off the wheel, and his wife is suing him for desertion. Last night he shouted: 'My legs are the same length.' A leading psychiatrist told me that in his view, the clown is an idiot.

———————————

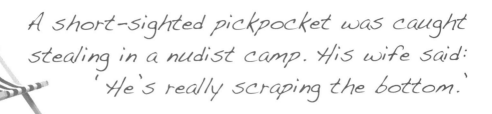

A short-sighted pickpocket was caught stealing in a nudist camp. His wife said: 'He's really scraping the bottom.'

The strike at the Pot Gnome Factory may well be tied up with the Mafia. An Italian dwarf who poses for pixie figurines was hit in the face with a bag of Dream Topping last night. Detectives are hunting for a man seen riding a pony in plus fours. A policeman said: 'You don't get many ponies wearing plus fours.'

A man who is colour blind went out last night and painted the town brown.

_____

Marvin Looe from Marton is to try and drink Windermere dry for charity. Last year you may recall, he chewed his way across the Pennines on his back and raised £11 for Sudanese orphans, and now suffers from soil erosion.

_____

Vindaloo curry has been found in vast quantities down a well in a plumber's backyard. Already the find is causing chaos with North Sea Curry shares. In Bombay, the news caused a riot among manure students and a fish and chip shop in the Ganges was swamped with ointment.

_____

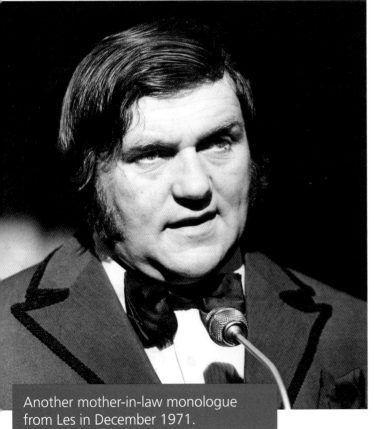

Another mother-in-law monologue from Les in December 1971.

11

"Dr" Les with stethoscope and curious TV show 'patient' in May 1969.

Police have issued an identikit of a pigmy who is being considered responsible for stuffing animals at Blackpool Zoo. A rare Ohio coyote was found in Stanley Park stuffed with river sand and wool, and now there are fears that a middle-aged jackass with a weight problem may have met the same fate. A spokesman for the zoo told me that the jackass hasn't moved an inch since Lent.

Roscoe Chip, the American who is accused of blowing eggs through his vest in Preston, took his clothes off in court today and a lady tattooist played a Himalayan flute as the judge fell asleep.

Q&A

Q What is your greatest fear?

A That prohibition might come back.

Q What is your greatest virtue?

A Fighting prohibition.

Q Where would you like to be now?

A A brewery.

Q How would you like to be remembered?

A With a hiccup.

Q What do you worry about?

A Thirst.

the Dawson Slant

12 August 1982

For culture buffs, the good news is that the Freckleton Royal Opera House is to re-open with a modern version of Grubb's immortal The Nude Trumpeter. Many of you will recall Madam Gertie Bugri singing the lament to her hunched aunt when she finds a mouse being sick in a parcel. For me, however, the moment to savour is when Gertie Bugri sees her deaf lover going bald in a cupboard.

Roscoe Chip, the American tourist who is accused of blowing eggs through his vest in Preston, was held in contempt by Judge Potter when he tried to whistle Mammy in Polish. The judge said afterwards that he was fed up with the trial and his back ached. Counsel for the defence today called three dwarfs to testify that Roscoe Chip was a supreme artiste and should be given a week's engagement at the North Pier and a free ticket for the Poulton Fish Festival.

The Fleetwood clown who lost his trousers on a ferris wheel still refuses to come down for his tea. A pair of jeans were dropped to him from a helicopter but they didn't fit and now the clown's shirt is coming apart at the seams. His wife is appealing for men to offer old trousers to cover his embarrassment. Meanwhile, the ferris wheel is jammed and no rescue can be effected. A man who used to be a stuntman for the Wooden Tops, has offered to climb up with a pair of shorts, but his father won't let him.

The North Sea Curry crisis goes on. In New Delhi, a maiden lady from Doncaster, whose parents used to ship tripe to Bengal, was found upside down in a brass tea urn with a sliver of madras chicken shoved up her nose. In the House of Commons, Sir Godfrey Belch condemned the incident and demanded action. Meanwhile, in Bradford, Ram Jam Fhull, the high commissioner for Indian affairs, warned the Government to stop people sucking curry up out of the sea, and said he would advise his government to ban exports of Eccles cakes.

There is grave concern at Blackpool Zoo over the discovery that a Madagascan fruit bat, which had refused food for a week, had in fact been stuffed with strands of kapok. A spokesman for the zoo said that it appeared that the bat had been used as an umbrella. Police are worried that there may be a link between the bat in Blackpool and an ostrich in Whipsnade that was found stuffed with sawdust in a lavatory. A pigmy is being sought for questioning in the macabre affair.

The balloon goes up in July 1986 as Blackpool's unstinting ambassador is announced as the Illumination's switch-on star.

A man who once claimed he had the tallest knees in the world died last week aged 89. For years he kept a permissive launderette in Warton and was popular with Arabs. He played the piano in a marching band and never suffered from boils. He has left his body to science and they are now contesting the will. He leaves a wife and a daughter aged 70 and she works on the Pleasure Beach.

Will Henry Gossett, last seen in a tattoo parlour in 1923, please contact his wife who is still waiting for him outside Central Pier.

The strike at the pot gnome factory goes into its third week. Already, overseas orders for clay fairies and glazed alabaster elves have been cancelled by the Uganda Ministry of Defence. Liverpool dockers have threatened to go on a work-to-rule if 15 crates of plastic imps and chrome-tipped pigeons aren't moved from a Liberian tanker. Chaos, remarked Emily Maggs as she knitted a cover for her Walter's commode.

Ever the joker, Les takes the plunge fancy dress style to officially open St Annes swimming baths in April 1987.

Starting today, by popular demand, a serialisation of Spencer Creambaum's novel: Earache In August.

The Ring Of The Camel

Inspector Coote filled his gnarled briar with dark shag and puffed reflectively. Sergeant Bustop filled his puff and gnarled his briared shag darkly. Coote reflectively briared and puffed his shagfilled gnarl. (Next week: *Omens*).

S wiss-born, Blackpool-based scientist, Doctor Helmut Clack, is at it again. Last night, before a mixed audience of lapsed Jesuits and embalmers, the old fool stated in a loud voice, that he could run a second-hand Morris on steamed fog and ferret droppings. A mechanic with a limp threw a lemon pie at the celebrated scientist, and two nuns mugged a tea blender.

———————————————

There is great excitement over the announcement that the Rossall Clock Mine is to re-open on Wednesdays. Mr Arthur Bagg, the man who discovered that people who ate prunes were never late for work, found a wrist watch and a fob time-piece down number one shaft. Many watches were mined from Rossall during the latter part of the century, but with the death of Sir Guy Cacklebottom in Nigeria in 1934 the mine was closed and turned into a cinema.

———————————————

the Dawson Slant

19 August 1982

A detachment of SAS troops are to be dropped by parachute in an effort to get the Fleetwood clown off the ferris wheel. You may recall that the clown lost his trousers a week ago, and refused to come down. Yesterday he was seen swinging his legs over the rim of the giant wheel and banging his head with a mallet. During a divorce hearing, his wife said that he'd always been peculiar and kept pancakes in a suitcase.

———————————

A set of dentures made out of Bulgarian onyx with tungsten-tipped molars were auctioned in Little Thornton last Friday. They had belonged to a gay hussar in Berlin who lost his foot on the Somme, and were a prize for his skill at varnishing Bovril lids for singers who'd gone deaf.

———————————

Police now know that the pygmy is responsible for stuffing various animals in Stanley Park Zoo. His ex-landlady, a Mrs Emily Wrench, told a detective that when he lodged with her, he stuffed her pet canary and a pensioner who used to borrow milk off her. "I thought it was funny at the time, like," Mrs Wrench stated. "The old man hadn't moved for a month and I couldn't Hoover the rug for 'im sprawled there. Anyway, I took his waistcoat and braces off to dust 'im, and cotton wool balls fell out of his ears. Queer, it was." Meanwhile, a cow in Poulton found propped up against a council worker was, on closer inspection, found to be well stuffed with wood chippings and Guinness labels.

Roscoe Chip, the American who blew eggs through his vest in Preston, was refused bail today after he admitted bribing two dwarfs to file evidence on his behalf. Judge Wimberry thundered in court: "This is not Detroit, you colonial rascal!"

———————————

Horsebottom Towers, home of the Potts-Belching family, is to be opened to the public. The Potts-Belchings were a strange lot: Sir Gideon Potts-Belching went mad in a bucket and his three sons married a homing pigeon for a jape. Lady Rowena Potts-Belching used to trap mice in her corsets and her husband wouldn't work if there was a Friday in the week. The stately home is a four-storey bungalow with 36 wooden lavatories. The main point of interest is the Gothic trumpet display near the hyena pit.

———————————

This and that: Dum Dum Pickle and his Hot Shot Turnip Band are in town. This heavy metal group who play violins made of iron have a record in the charts and a couple of hernias.

Les Dawson and the Roly Polys line up at Blackpool Grand Theatre in 1984.

the Dawson Slant

26 August 1982

And now ... Continuing our serialisation of Spencer Creambaum's novel: Earache In August.

Omens

Once again, Inspector Coote filled his gnarled briar with dark shag and puffed reflectively as he confronted Lady Akkers. Sergeant Busstop akkered his gnarl and puffed his shag as he filled. Lady Akkers lit a cigar and coughed. Inspector Coote, reflectively lit and gnarled his shagged briar. Lady Akkers cigarred her gnarl and lit a reflective as Sergeant Busstop lit his akkers and gnarled his shag as he filled and puffed. (Next week: Threads)

I have been approached to include in this column the works of the Lytham Poet, Fred Crunchbuckle. Fred, who had a friend in the ballet, lived all his life in a tool shed and drank only carrot juice. It used to make him drunk, but he could see better. He never married and spent a lot of time at scout jamborees. For years he had trouble with his nose and he couldn't wear sandals.

He liked to sit on sheep and he could imitate a water lily. He was a shy man and when he died, his hearse followed the mourners. I have taken the liberty of reproducing below his most famous poem, once considered a masterpiece in Todmorden massage parlours:

Rolling leas and hooded woods,
Shining brook, reflecting buds.
Gather the roses, take a pick -
And behind a thicket, a cat is sick.

A few words from Les at the switch-on of the Illuminations in August 1991.

Cranford Bottle, the Halifax agent who handles Martha Hagget's Trombone Romany Band, told me that Plumm refused to appear at the Gaiety, Ayr, with Moon's Jumping Infants until they were 21 and wearing scarves.

North sea curry is to be sold in chip shops, and that is official. The crisis worsened yesterday, with the news that Hindu caterers were about to invade Bolton, and 300 Bengal poppadum fryers are marching across Garstang burning every lamb chop in sight. Ram Jam Fhull, the Indian Minister of Affairs, has stated openly that North Sea Curry is a threat to the stability of the Far East, and a backbencher smacked his legs with a box of apricots.

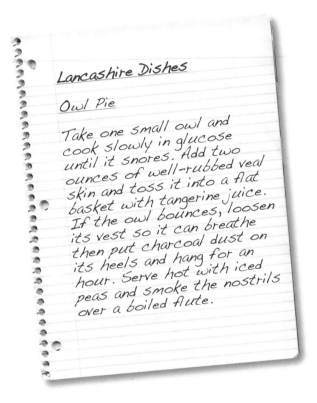

Lancashire Dishes

Owl Pie

Take one small owl and cook slowly in glucose until it snores. Add two ounces of well-rubbed veal skin and toss it into a flat basket with tangerine juice. If the owl bounces, loosen its vest so it can breathe then put charcoal dust on its heels and hang for an hour. Serve hot with iced peas and smoke the nostrils over a boiled flute.

My news of the recovery from illness of Max Plumm, the old variety artiste, has brought a flood of mail in. From Lambert Goose, the underwater ventriloquist exponent and talking mind-reader, comes a story of Max working with Johnson's Catholic Ferrets at the Liver Clinic and Thermal Baths, Crewe. It appears that one of the ferrets fell into a stripper's bathtub whilst the lady was performing the nude stick dance, and although the ferret was lost, she had an angelic smile on her face all week.

———————————

Three lions were found stuffed with breadcrumbs and rice in Blackpool Zoo by a girl guide with acne. A spokesman hiding in an antelope's sleeping bag told me that nothing moves very much in the zoo now, and that the mere mention of the dreaded pygmy sends the staff scurrying for safety. A golfer at Fairhaven who had not left a bunker in a fortnight was found to be crammed to his gills with kapok and glue. Police are intensifying their search for the murderous little native who is thought to be carrying a sand wedge in his loincloth.

The Swiss-born, Blackpool-based scientist, Dr Helmut Clack, blew a fisherman's hat off yesterday, with an explosive acorn. The fisherman, who wouldn't give his name, said that the good doctor had tried to get rid of a wart under his (the fisherman's) wig without upsetting the parting of the toupee. Dr Clack stated that very soon now, he'd have perfected a vacuum cleaner for getting rid of dandruff on puff adders.

———————————

The old Lakeland sport of squirrel groping is to be revived at long last, and I for one, rejoice. To see men dressed in the traditional garb of Inverness capes and see-through gaiters sliding along on baked mud rafts, is a sight to linger on the mind. A well-groped squirrel lives longer and never suffers from gallstones.

———————————

Muscle man Les showing off by the side of his outdoor pool just two weeks after his move to Islay Road, Lytham, after living in Bury for ten years.

"I keep discovering rooms I didn't even know existed. Even the mice wear St Christopher medals."

Continued now chapter three of the novel: Earache In August.

Threads

Inspector Coote sniffed and filled his gnarled briar with dark shag and puffed reflectively as he spoke to the Prussian maid. Sergeant Busstop sniffed his shag and reflectively gnarled as he puffed his fill with a Prussian briar. The maid gnarled and puffed with a briared shag and reflectively sniffed the dark. Next week: *Tulips*

F our red ladies with ginger beards attacked Roscoe Chip in court today. Chip, accused of blowing eggs through his vest in Preston, had just painted his nostrils with onion fat to get a laugh, when the women started smacking his head with a bag of Patna rice. Judge Cackle threw his wig through the window and had the women put in a billiard hall. The case continues.

_____

Horror upon horror, gentle reader, but I have to inform you that the final resting place of Albert Ackroyd, last of the Southport vampires, was found today. You may recall that Albert was killed with a sliver of frozen black tripe, hammered through his vile heart. Although he had no teeth, he could suck a cow to death and so great was the suction, he once hung from Tesco's window by his gums for an hour. His wife Annie ran away from him in the Isle of Man when he grabbed two midgets. She told me: "He got nasty when he drank shorts."

_____

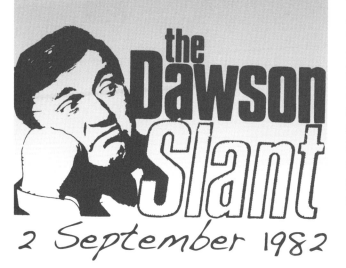

the Dawson Slant

2 September 1982

The Fleetwood clown who lost his trousers on a ferris wheel still refuses to come down and last night he started to unravel his underpants. A pair of leather Alpine shorts were thrown up to him and he ate them with whipped cream and cabbage.

A tattooed monk with money in the Post Office tried to entice a seagull on a Co-op ledge with a packet of wafer biscuits late last night. When arrested, he steadfastly refused to say why he'd done it and asked the officer in charge could he sing Mammy for charity.

The old variety act The Masked Gurkha's and Winnie is to be recreated by Weinbeck and Finklebaum, the Jewish comedy duo who surrendered to Rommel in Chiswick. This will come as a shock to Max Plumm, who was with the original act when it played the Freckleton Royal Opera House before Count Gustave Von Spitz and his wife Jean. Max was not available today for comment. His wife said he was having a drink at the vets.

The Swiss-born, Blackpool-based scientist, Dr Helmut Clack, has startled the world with his discovery that if a cat gives birth in a bowler hat, the kittens could grow up round-shouldered. Speaking through his shirt, he told a conference of nudists that bending horses was dangerous as well. He really is a remarkable man.

Concern is growing over the fate of middle-aged whelks in Liverpool. Apparently silt rising from the ocean floor gives them myopia and backache, not to mention colon problems. Now there is a demand for prawns to wear knickers in cold weather.

Ladies! Don't suffer crow's feet - wear socks! If you have flat feet, don't worry about it. Buy a food pump. Do you want people to look up to you when you die? Be buried in a tree. Cross a goat with an owl and have a hootnanny!

It seems certain now that Morecambe will be turned into an intensive care unit for tourists. A man who was found breathing in Heysham was deported back to Tintwistle for loitering with intent to live.

Searching for inspiration during the opening of Kirkham Grammar School's Sports Day in September 1980.

Q&A

Q What is your biggest fault?

A What's a fault?

Q Who do you most admire?

A Coronation flag sellers.

Q What annoys you?

A People who set out these bloody questionnaires.

Q What is your ambition?

A To go round the world one year and somewhere different the next.

Chapter four of our stirring serial from the book: Earache in August.

Tulips

Inspector Goote filled his gnarled briar with dark shag and puffed reflectively as he sized up the winsome parlour maid. Sergeant Busstop winsomely gnarled his puff and parloured dark size with a reflective shag. The parlour maid filled a winsome size with a dark puff and reflectively gnarled a briared shag with an up.

Next: *Murder In The Font.*

It now looks as if Garstang is going ahead with plans for home rule. Ever since the discovery of North Sea Curry, the inhabitants of Garstang have become increasingly hostile to the rest of Lancashire, and now, all roads into Garstang are closed and passports are demanded before entry. "We can field an army of a hundred if necessary," shouted General Catchpole Fogg to our reporter, who had beans thrown at his waistcoat by a youth on a skateboard. Last night, an armed detachment of the Garstang Mounted Foot Brigade, shot a Morecambe poacher up his duffle bag, and a crazed otter bit his lip.

the Dawson Slant

9 September 1982

Swiss-born, Blackpool-based scientist, Doctor Helmut Clack, has invented electric braces for people with tall knees. Following my article about the man from Warton who claimed to have the tallest knees in the world, the good doctor made a painstaking investigation into this knotty problem and came up with some quite astounding data. For instance; people with tall knees never eat radishes nor can they comb their hair whilst standing on the arm of a sofa. Special knickers were tried out in Sweden for tall-kneed women, but the drawers caused them to lean to the left. Dr Clack believes his motorised braces are the answer ... a small battery-driven one-phase motor is fitted in the gusset of a pair of jockey shorts, then a fan belt is screwed tight up the armpit and threaded into a socket on the braces. Early test show that the cut-out switch doesn't always work and the trousers go over the head and cause panic among the middle-aged. But at least the problem is being pursued.

A first night audience at the Freckleton Royal Opera House gave Madam Gerta Bugri, the Milan diva, a standing ovation after she had sung the aria from Serge Whaleborne's composition, *Die Flugel Finsdepuffen*. Madam Gerta, playing the role of Caspar, the ferret strangler in a leper colony, won her applause when she carried a horse along a length of fuse wire.

The Fleetwood clown who lost his trousers on a ferris wheel is now wearing asbestos curtains and is eating toffee.

Marvin Looe, the man who attempted to drink Windermere for charity is recovering in Lancaster. Undaunted by his ordeal, Mr Looe now plans to eat a tree to raise money for ruptured apes in the Congo delta.

Roscoe Chip, the American who is accused of blowing eggs through his vest in Preston, entertained a packed courtroom by bouncing a rubber crumpet off the judge's wig. A man with a tape recorder in his sandal was removed after he tried to put a piece of rump in a dwarf's handbag. (Case continues.)

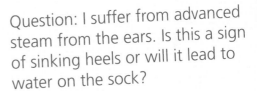

Doctor Rhubarb's Corner

Question: I suffer from advanced steam from the ears. Is this a sign of sinking heels or will it lead to water on the sock?

Answer: Steam coming from the ears is not always a good sign and it won't get you a seat on a bus. However if you iron the lower thighs and eat plenty of fish manure with coleslaw you should be able to yodel in a tin.

Les at the piano tells another rib-tickling tale in January 1986.

"On his off-key piano style, Les said: "It's nice to know that people can detect true genius when they hear it. I was self taught - no one else would teach me.""

At last dear reader, the final episode of our serialisation of the novel: Earache In August...

Finale

Inspector Coote filled his gnarled briar with dark shag and puffed reflectively as Lord Botty sipped a rich ruby with great elan. Sergeant Busstop gnarled his ruby and briared his shag with a puff reflectively as he filled his sip. Lord Botty sipped his shag and puffed his gnarl with a dark reflective puff and gnarled his ruby... I'm fed up now.

D id you know that if you inject a turnip with influenza it will attack a bath mat? Are you aware that if you shove suet up a monk's kilt during a cold spell his cassock will self-destruct? Did you know that if you shoot the eyebrows off a trout whilst it is mating, you will never suffer from dandruff of the knuckle? Astounding is it not?

But one man knew all these things: Otlis P. Clout, the Runcorn Memory Man. All next week he is appearing under the Central Pier with a Danish juggler who juggles with lentils in an accordion, and a troupe of stunted Polish Morris Dancers. Admission is free if you're over seven and married to an orphan.

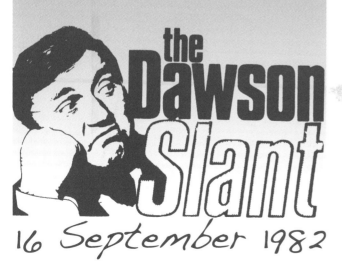

the **Dawson Slant**

16 September 1982

More news of the Pot Gnome strike. Six boxes of glazed imps were drip dried in a potter's kiln and were ruined. Missing, also from stock, are 29 rubber fawns, ten comical elves with long chins and a clay flamingo in burnt cerise. A dwarf who models for fishpond gnomes, is being sought by the police for deliberately gluing a papier-mâché fairy prince to a stone mongoose.

The Rossall Clock Mine is in the news today. Work started on number three shaft where, it is believed, wrist watches and alarm clocks are in abundance. Two clock miners drilled through a strata of fossilised lime rock and dinosaur dung, and found three second fingers and a brass weight.

" The wife plays trombone in bed – I don't like it because it's chipping the paint off my harp."

Happy and relaxed in April 1986.

The Government is seriously concerned about Garstang's determination to enforce home rule, and tanks are being made at Airfix to combat the threat. General Fogg, at his headquarters in a brewery, thundered to the local radio interviewer that his army was ready to take anybody on, then sang Nellie Dean to a friend of Hughie Green.

A new film based on the life of a man whose wife gave birth to an ostrich, is to be shown later this year at Bispham. It is a moving film that covers the life of the man from his early days spent in a box of muffins, to his time as a misk ox gall bladder specialist in Rotherham. Lena Gosling plays his wife. She recently starred in Adam's Teeth Are Itching the movie that was shot under a quilt in a bog. The scene where a dying whippet chokes on a pickle will have the handkerchiefs out.

Les Dawson launched his very own celebrity golf tournament at Fairhaven GC in March 1982. Among the sporting greats who took part were Sir Matt Busby and Gordon Banks.

Blackpool Zoo is in dire trouble. It was revealed yesterday that the nude pygmy in a bowler hat and pants has finally stuffed all the animals there. A small orangutan, which has been hanging for a week from a plastic banyan bush, fell off during the night and shredded wheat poured from its nostrils. Fears are growing for the safety of a coach load of Nottingham pensioners who are missing on a moorland road near Bakewell. An unemployed shepherd from Lambeth told a traffic warden he'd sighted the pigmy eating a banana in Buxton.

A woman who claimed that wearing an iron hat gave her bad feet, fell off a tram today whilst plucking a rabbit. Her brother, who's just won a teapot and a set of zinc acorns in a Scrabble contest, said he thought his sister was too young to shave, and shut the shed door in our reporter's face.

Quite the gent – Les dons a tweed trilby in this stern portrait picture taken in September 1982.

the **Dawson** Slant

23 September 1982

Are the Cubans in Garstang? Reports being sent to us by a hairdresser who used to play a bugle in the SAS would suggest that Castro sent 15,000 troops in registered envelopes to aid Garstang's fight for Home Rule. General Fogg, at his headquarters in a brewery, denied the allegation before he passed out, and said they were merely relatives of Minnie, the woman he lives with over a windmill.

A boiled owl in a check cap found stuffed in a polythene truss, is to be auctioned next week in Poulton-le-Fylde. A man who was trapped for three days in a vacuum cleaner found the owl when his wife emptied him into a bin liner. A spokesman for the British Museum said that in his view the owl was worthless unless kept in grease-proof paper under a haversack.

Roscoe Chip, the American who is accused of blowing eggs through his vest in Preston, ate his shoes in court today. The judge, who was arm wrestling a black midget for money, had Chip handcuffed to an insurance salesman who is charged with wallpapering Pontins.

That insane, nude pigmy in a bowler hat and spats, has created yet another horror to chill our blood. The coach load of Nottingham pensioners missing on the Derbyshire moors, have been found....yes, stuffed with burnt hay. An official at the Gas Board discovered them as he was jogging with his friend, Julian. Ten of the pensioners were hanging out to dry from an elm branch, which gives rise to speculation that the pigmy was disturbed by someone or something.

Historic Lancashire

Five miles from Kirkham as the crow coughs, lies the village of Ruff-on-the-Ole. The village is so far off the beaten track, Dracula got in for the Liberals. It's a poor village, in fact the wishing well is full of IOUs. All the inhabitants are closely intermarried, and they take it in turns to be the village idiot. It's a very old fashioned hamlet, there is only one store, and it's called: 'A Do It Thy Self Shoppe'. The only industry is the traditional trade of warthog welding. Cromwell is supposed to have watered his horse there, and the smell still lingers. Nearby is the ruin of a Tudor brothel and harp discount centre. The local cemetery is of interest to brass rubbing enthusiasts and Bovril is served on Thursdays.

There is to be, at last I might add, an investigation into the goings on at Mrs Wrench's guesthouse. A holidaymaker who escaped from the guesthouse, disguised as a nun, told stunned policemen of the things Mrs Wrench gets up to. Apparently, a nice couple from Ormskirk, whose daughter mends dominoes, asked Mrs Wrench for another piece of bacon grill. They'd no sooner said it, when Mrs Wrench attacked them with a buzz saw and threw some amputated bits to her canary. There is talk of digging up the backyard of the guesthouse to find the remains of an architect who once complained that his cocoa was tepid. Gossip has it that Mrs Wrench strangled him with corset elastic. For years I have badgered the authorities to confront Mrs Wrench, because in 1953, she walled my Aunt Jean up for asking for a slice of winberry flan.

Doctor Rhubarb's Corner

Question: When my husband swallowed a toffee pig during the war, his tonsils were lagged with crepe squares and he lay for an hour up a funnel. I think he's dead but my mother keeps on ironing him. What should I do?

Answer: Unplug the iron and watch for him gargling with soda ash. If he crosses his legs under the left ear put him in an overcoat daubed with wax and then screw his head in a basinful of lupin juice.

Les with good friend and fellow golf fanatic Frank Carson in April 1982

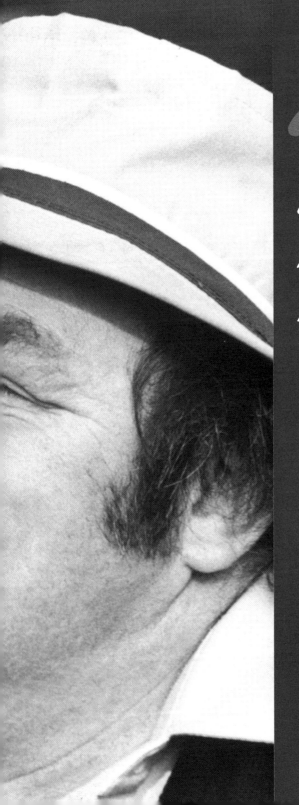

"What talent would you most like to have?

To interrupt Frank Carson."

the Dawson Slant

30 September 1982

Mrs Wrench, the South Shore guesthouse keeper, kept police at bay yesterday with a blunderbuss and a set of Peruvian blow pipes. Mrs Wrench is accused of slaughtering well over 100 holidaymakers who stayed at the guesthouse. The remains of a couple were found shoved under a floorboard in a bath house extension, they were named as Mr and Mrs Cromford. MacRobbie, missing since 1964. A woman who once worked for Mrs Wrench was seen climbing into the MacRobbie's room with a Bowie knife and a steel-tipped mallet.

Interpol wish to interview Mrs Wrench regarding the disappearance of a French sanitary engineer who couldn't eat black tripe. According to a window cleaner, who would not reveal his name, he witnessed Mrs Wrench trying to force a strip of tripe down the Frenchman's throat, crying as she did: "It cost good money this, you damn frog." Later the window cleaner said he heard a muffled scream followed by the sound of a high-speed drill. Meanwhile, the cellar floor is being dug up, and a labourer gave in his notice when an arm shot up from the hole in the concrete.

The Fleetwood clown who lost his trousers on a ferris wheel, allowed a tattoist to climb up and ink in a strand of mistletoe on his left buttock. The clown's ex-wife fired an air gun pellet at her estranged partner and then tried to siphon petrol from a tractor. A mountaineer is to be hired to clamber up the steel work in an effort to grab the clown, who is being accused of lowering the rateable value of Coral Island.

North Sea Curry shares fell yet again on the Stock Exchange when it was revealed that, if taken in large doses, it can cause high blood pressure and rot a person's surgical appliance. The Indian Minister for Foreign Affairs, Mr Ram Jam Fhull, said in Bradford today that only a genuine curry would suffice for the heavily incontinent. Three men with sticks were fined for sucking up the curry off the North Pier without a licence.

Les took a trip down the aisle for the second time in less than 18 months, for the wedding of his eldest daughter Julie in September 1990.

A cavalry charge failed to break through the defences that have been constructed across the main road into Garstang. Garstang, which is demanding Home Rule, declared triumphantly that they took six prisoners and a lame mule into custody, and General

Foff – at his headquarters in a brewery – said he intended to ask Vera Lynn to sing at his brother's wedding. The Cuban troops in Garstang have been reinforced by a lorry load of depressed Scarborough hoteliers, who want Freddie Trueman to be the Yorkshire ambassador to Garstang. Fred wasn't available for comment.

In Town This Week

Franz Noodle, the German brick hypnotist at the Ansdell Institute. who once sent a bungalow to sleep in Weymouth, is over here to attempt to put St Annes under the influence... frankly that shouldn't take much doing.

In Cleveleys, for a limited season, is the Jorace School of Musical Stomachs. They've just returned from a pith helmet factory in Haslingden. There is a glass eye exhibition in the foyer of the Imperial Hotel next Tuesday, and that should see them through until the week after.

Swiss-born, Blackpool-based scientist, Doctor Helmut Clack, gave a Press interview today in order to show his electric braces for people with tall knees. Frankly it was a trifle disappointing because the model used, a hairless eunuch from Rhyl, had bandy legs and the trousers snagged halfway down and the battery-driven motor blew up. There was trouble also with the fan belt as it revolved and the man's dentures were pulled out when the belt flew off the pulley wheel. Dr Clack refused to comment on the farce and made rude comments about Michael Foot.

Swiss-born, Blackpool-based scientist, Doctor Helmut Clack, is to be hauled up before the courts following complaints from the government of the new African state of Uh Mah Bumm. It appears that the good doctor sold the natives 300 of his electric braces which were used to hold up the trousers of the new state's army. During a pitched battle in a rain forest, the battery-driven motors became damp, and the soldiers had to charge with their pants three foot above their heads. They blundered blindly into a swamp, and a colonel was eaten by an outraged hippo. From evidence sifted, it would seem the cut-out switch on the shoulder blade burns to a clinker when the fan belt whips off the socket up the armpit. Dr Clack was not available for comment yesterday; his assistant said he was in Bognor having a sandwich.

The Fleetwood clown who lost his trousers on a ferris wheel made an attempt to climb down this morning but a bald hooligan peppered the clown's buttocks with dried peas, and he's back up the wheel again. Oxfam are to send garments to the poor soul to cover his dignity. "After all, people laugh at little things like that," remarked his wife in Miami.

There are so many people in Garstang now that cramp is a big problem. Nobody smiles anymore because there isn't enough room to do it, and nose blowing is banned.

---

the Dawson Slant

7 October 1982

April 1988. As patron of the Victoria Hospital Scanner Appeal, Les was always on hand to say thanks for a donation.

A preservation order is to be slapped on a Miss Agatha Loome whose foot suffered an earthquake last year. Miss Loome sits on hot fish for a living and knits freckles for a joke shop.

Les raises a glass to good friends Mo Moreland and husband Roy who celebrated their silver wedding anniversary in August 1984.

That bloody pigmy is at it again! A small boy who complained to his mother that his donkey wouldn't shift on the sands, had to be heavily sedated with chocolate after the wee lad pulled handfuls of seaweed from a hole in the animals head. A police spokesman said sternly that if the pigmy in the bowler hat and spats is not apprehended soon, nothing will move in Lancashire. To date, the lunatic has stuffed five tigers, three lions, a fruit bat, six elephants and a kangaroo, a coach load of pensioners, three tourists and a hunched monk. Also it is believed he is behind the stuffing of a lame wrestler from Ealing, the man's sister, and an accountant who once went out with Flora Robson.

Book review

Rhubarb Squints by Heather Tickle. The sobering tale of a man who discovered the source of the M6 whilst sandpapering his wife's crutch for a marathon hop. Sad in parts and full of splinters.

So great was the response to my article on traditional Lancashire dishes, I have taken the liberty of setting down for your appraisal, details of that tasty repast.

Lancashire Dishes

Old Horse Soup

Take one elderly horse that sweats in fog, peel and add an onion that's been rolled in a khaki hat. Find a large bowl and bend the fetlocks until the saddle makes a noise. Add a pinch of buttered stoat nostril and stir until it whistles. Boil in a bag of oats for an hour then weld a lid on the stirrups. Serve with freshly-greased peanuts and burnt cider.

It is known in government circles that not only are the Cubans in Garstang, but also 25,000 Catholic Arabs as well. Garstang is determined to have self-rule and the town council are building a ten-foot wall all around the place. General Fogg, at his headquarters in a brewery, said he now has an army of 50,000 men, but only one gun which is on lease from a Confederate museum in Alabama.

In town for a limited season under the North Pier is Cissie Goose and her all-bearded accordian band. Last seen on the Fylde during the war, the band, which plays on stilts, entertained Army deserters in Russia. Miss Goose herself once breathed on Marley tiles for a bet, and she's full of fun. For me, the highlight of the night is when the band bang their knuckles with tent pegs and do impressions of a warped gate.

Q&A

Q What is your favourite food/drink?

A All of it.

Q What is your favourite music?

A "Drink To Me Only".

Q What is your favourite book?

A Anthology of pubs through the ages.

Garstang has asked the Japanese not to send any more troops. General Fogg, at his headquarters in a brewery has give way to the town council, who are worried about the lack of oxygen brought on by the impact of the arrival of 15,000 Dutch mountain cavalry and 1,600 Japanese hari kari advisors. A note smuggled out from Garstang tells of the hardship endured by the inhabitants who are breathing in and out by numbers. Things could get worse. The Gazette, always ahead with the news, has information that 3,000 troops from Borneo are on the way to help Garstang in the struggle for Home Rule. Personally, I think it's daft.

Historic Lancashire

Cobham's Hole: One of the oldest holes in Britain, it was formally used as a Regency cats' retreat for doctored toms that couldn't readjust. It's a deep hole and Cromwell had a habit of throwing up in it. Dickens was said to have used it as a lavatory and the caretaker in it now, remembers the time Vera Lynn dropped a haddock down the hole to get her voice back. On Tuesday you can see the Dance of the Preston Virgins round the hole and take photographs of liver.

the Dawson Slant

14 October 1982

Les couldn't wait to pucker up for the cameras and the crowds after his marriage to Tracy in 1989.

More corpses have been found in the guesthouse belonging to Mrs Wretch. Police unearthed the remains of a family slaughtered when they asked for another kipper. A relative who travelled down from Dundee told the authorities she received a telephone call from the dead family the night before the kipper incident and they begged her to send a good parcel. Meanwhile the diggings in the cellar have produced the bodies of 14 Boy Scouts who once stayed at the guesthouse. A man who used to clean the Boy Scouts woggles, said the lads had irritated Mrs Wretch by stealing spoonfuls of mashed potato. A lump in the back garden turned out to be the burial mound of a commercial traveller who dared to ask Mrs Wretch for more mushy peas. Mrs Wretch is hiding on the roof at the present time, and keeps throwing slates at the police. We've just heard that a body has been found in the water cistern of the guesthouse, heavily decomposed. (Not the body, the cistern.)

_____

WANTED

Contact lens for a household oyster, any price.

Marvin Looe, who ate a tree for charity, is suffering now from an acorn rash, with suspected Dutch Elm disease. Undaunted though, he still intends to go ahead with plans to lick the Preston by-pass. His mother is very worried and she's got trouble with her back.

Freckleton Royal Opera House is to stage the First World War on ice. Madam Gerta Bugri will sing the title role of Hindenburg who gets bilious during a clarinet lesson, and Senor Phillipe Mucho, whose father was a prawn salesman in Oldham, will sing with his shoulder against a dead hare. Madame Gerta hasn't been well after falling off a walrus and her nose is still blocked with wood. North Sea Curry is running out and that's a fact. Only two buckets of the stuff were raised last week off Fleetwood and it was cold as well. Test boring on Marton Moss shows that Madras curry is plentiful enough but full of frogs. On the stock exchange, a speculator who'd lost his shirt on the deal, went mad and bit a ventriloquist on the Pleasure Beach. The Indian Government is delighted, of course, and are resuming the sale of muffins to camel drovers.

Swiss-born, Blackpool-based scientist, Doctor Helmut Clack has invented yet another boon for mankind: musical gas-fired socks for shy people. The idea is a simple one: Timid folk who find conversations with other people difficult, can now break the ice by putting on a pair of socks on say a tram, and play a tune for the passengers. This will get them talking and make them better citizens. A small gas cylinder is fastened between the legs and this rotates a button which then switches on the music tape as the socks are pulled up … interesting, hey?

Doctor Rhubarb's Corner

Question: Is it possible to get coloured headaches after chewing a brass cradle? My husband says no but he's a funny shape to start with and wants to marry a seal. I've started drinking from a tool kit and my ears are loose..

Answer: Brass cradles are dangerous if not coated with salmon hairs, but coloured headaches are rare unless you've pickled your teeth in jam. Try threading your head with rubber screws then suck a pair of pliers dry in a box of grass.

Les tees off in inimitable style for the 16th Les Dawson Golf Tournament in May 1991.

Why take up golf, Les was asked in September 1986. "Well the dog died," he joked.

The Fairhaven Lake monster has been sighted yet again, and this time the report comes from an unimpeachable source. Mrs Emily Gwaine-Gust, whose husband is a high Court advocate and amateur glassblower, saw the humped serpent rise from the water as she was practising her yoga in a skiff.

"It has a rather elongated neck," Mrs Gwaine-Gust told me.

"The head has some sort of horny things sticking out from behind its ears, and I heard it break wind!" the dear old lady swooned and was hurried off to the Old Bank Tea Shop for a stiff shot of home-brewed bourbon. It was way back in 1923 that a certain Leeds dentist was dragged under the waters of Fairhaven. The dentist was never seen again, and with the insurance his wife bought a bungalow in Rhyl and grew dwarf oaks until she choked on a pickle.

The sighting of the monster is being played down by all the night-club owners in Ansdell because they say it will frighten gamblers out of the village. As Ansdell has long been considered the Las Vegas of the Coast, I can see their point of view.

All this is apart from hill tribesmen from Nepal who are over here to be fitted with National Health Sandals. Accommodation is nil, and the soldiers are standing on top of one another waiting to charge. People no longer walk on the pavements, they shuffle in groups of six, and very soon jumping on the spot will be banned.

the Dawson Slant

21 October 1982

Les with Roly Poly Mo Moreland

Clowning around with June Whitfield and Isla St Clair.

The Home Rule For Garstang Campaign is weakening, and that is official. General Fogg said today, from under a bar stool in his brewery headquarters, that there were now so many soldiers in the town, cramp was a big problem. "There are," he said between grins, "over 300,000 troops plus a Lebanese brass and a Riff flute ensemble here, and tomorrow we can expect a further 5,000 cadets from West Point."

Do-it-yourself Corner

Making a cork hat is simple enough. You need good quality cork and a strong stomach. Thread eel knee sinews through a clawed needle and tie off on a weaver's stitch. Place head in model basket and go home.

Lancashire Dishes

Corned Whippet Flan

First bake the whippet's head in a bag of raisins and rotate the paws with a fender. Take an ounce of well-shaken walnuts and squeeze them through a seasonal loofah. Push until broken and boil in hot lettuce water for an hour, then smack a bowl of chewed herbs with a stick until the whole thing stirs. Stand back with a burnt apron and spit soya beans on to a bed of shaved rice. Roll it up a hill and drop it in a garage until it sets. Serve with milk and lie down with a gooseberry.

The South Shore boarding house belonging to the infamous Mrs Wretch, has been the focus of police activity once more. Seven bodies have been found stuffed up a chimney in bin liners and a corpse was discovered in a chest freezer. A lapsed Freemason who once gave a lecture at the boarding house, remembers the seven people who demanded extra toast and jam during the Easter period and Mrs Wretch went for their throats. The body in the chest freezer has not been identified as yet, but a part-time waitress who worked for Mrs Wretch told reporters he looked like "the little chap wot asked for extra mushrooms on 'is steak." A police doctor said the man had been strangled with piano wire then burnt with a wielding kit. Meanwhile, Mrs Wretch is still on the roof and throwing offal at the policemen. We've just heard that another body, that of a parson who once asked for a water bottle, has been taken out of a cardboard box.

Q&A

Q What is your favourite/ and least favourite TV programme?

A Never awake long enough to tell.

Q Which actor, or actress, do you like?

A The one who gets the next round in.

Q What newspapers do you read?

A Lundy Isle Clarion, The Tonga Bugle, The Dandy and yours if I'm in it.

the **Dawson** *Slant*

28 October 1982

Since my startling exposé of the Fairhaven Lake Monster, six nude review shows in Ansdell have refused me admittance. (Not that I'm bothered; my eyesight was failing a bit).

Three casinos in Ansdell no longer allow me credit and to top it all, those great strippers, Fifi and Boom Boom Latour have stopped my afternoon sessions. The truth must be heard... there is something in that brooding lake and I demand, yet again, an investigation. I have written evidence that a grotesque creature with a long neck, big ears and a set of spotted legs lives under the turgid surface. It rises only to blow its nose and break wind and will eat anything that moves. Letters are pouring in, my friends, from bereaved relatives of missing holidaymakers. At random, here are just two of said missives...

Dear Sir or Madam
Mr Harry took a motor boat out on the lake in 1933 and he never came home and his tea was burnt. All they found were his trousers and a set of his old teeth. I've re-married but Harry had the back door key and the front door carpet is wearing out.
Cynthia Gloo (Staffs)

Dear Surr
In 1959 mi antie Jean was sat eating a potted befe sandwich with her feet in the lake at Fareavon. Blow me if i didn't see her been dragged into the water by the legs. Our dog Willie went in an rescuked Jean but not befor somthing had chewed half her bum off. She's never bin the same since and last week she bit a milkman's orse.
P. Smith (Jesus College, Oxford)

FOR SALE

One pair of antique camel's clogs with beaded lining. Made in Eccles by Smock and Sons in 1801. Were a gift to a baker from the Sudan who had a flat in Hammersmith. Puce lace on crimped leatherette give a gentle sweep to the wrought iron heels and embossed nails. Used only twice on a retired camel that had gone dry after a stroll. they make an investment and you can keep watercress in them.

The home rule for Garstang struggle took on an unpleasant aspect this morning. There are so many soldiers and suchlike in the town that food has become scarce and cannibalism is now strongly suspected. A well-meaning health food salesman crept into Garstang to promote a new pill that is said to grow ginseng on bald heads. The following morning his trilby hat was found in a makeshift oven and there was a distinct smell of chutney, plus a smear of Branston. To make matters worse the United Nations have sent over 9,000 Swedish troops and Bradford is to fly in a Punjab Morris Dancing Troupe.

A jar of North Sea Curry was sent to Swiss-born, Blackpool-based scientist Doctor Helmut Clack for analysis Dr Clack tasted it and declared the horse was unfit for work.

Roscoe Chip, the American who is accused of blowing eggs through his vest in Preston, shoved a tom cat up the judge's shirt yesterday. Two kilted steel workers held a man down who threatened Roscoe Chip with a week's cabaret at the Central Working Men's Club and he was hustled from the court crying: "Randolph Scott's a pouffe."

Doctor Rhubarb's Corner

Question: My niece swallowed a live duck and she coughs feathers in a tin. We've oiled her knees with suet but she keeps falling off caravans when she chases prawns. What can we do to stop her singlet from sticking to bricks?

Answer: Difficult one. If the duck is cross-eyed it will bite only on Thursday afternoons. Try rubbing her shins with a domino and keep her in a van. Take the singlet to a nude midget and let him draw sheep on the hem. Prawns are tricky to catch at the best of times and should be dipped in soup before they go on a roof.

"Ever joking, Les admitted in October 1991 he was a light eater: "Oh yes. As soon as it's light I start eating".

Les and Mo measure up in 1985.

the Dawson Slant

4 November 1982

In answer to the critics who accuse me of taking a very parochial view in this column, here are some world headlines:

The Hong Kong Bugle - A blue man with big ears who once did an impression of a wing-nut told a nude hypnotist on a raft, that his father was a bricklayer from Mars. He then lifted both legs off the ground and sang to his knees.

Bombay Gazette - A masked fireman in a wooden urinal took a Vauxhall tyre spanner from a German trout engineer and shoved it down a culvert.

Rio Observer - Two friends who boiled a tandem to prove a point, admitted that they had invented a Braille vest for their mother who teaches whelks to whistle.

———————————————

The home Rule for Garstang struggle is over. Yesterday, General Fogg reported that his brewery headquarters had run out of ale and the massed Cuban string orchestra was getting on his nerves. Lorryloads of soldiers are streaming out of the town and the rates are going up. All the Japanese troops have left and are now selling video sets from a hand cart in Morecambe. "It's a mess," said a councillor whose wife turned out to be a deserter from the Sudan.

———————————————

Les sees double outside Blackpool's Grand Theatre.

That great comedy duo from the days of variety, Weinbeck and Finkelbaum, are to publish their book of humour in the spring. Weinbeck and Finkelbaum were not Jewish. In fact a tree fell on them, and they surrendered to Rommel in Chiswick. I have taken the liberty of setting down some of the jokes that kept the nation in tears:

Weinbeck: "Why did the chicken cross the road?"

Finkelbaum: "I don't know" (This used to get howls)

Weinbeck: "Because it's Wednesday" (hoots).

Weinbeck: "I wouldn't say my wife's fat … but she is…. (roars).

Finkelbaum: "My wife is so thin, when she has a bath I weigh her down" (hysterics).

A concert in aid of a midget who's become a condensed milkman, raised over £20 and will be put towards a deaf aid for his pony who was saved from the knacker's yard by Miss Amy Lemon, the Poulton tea-blender and oil cloth varnisher.

Swiss-born, Blackpool-based scientist, Doctor Helmut Clack, has made several adjustments to his electric braces for people with tall knees. Now, instead of the single phase motor being screwed to the armpit, it will not dangle from a neck strap and the fan belt will be threaded down a pair of iced socks and fastened to a rawplug on the small toe. This makes it easier to switch on the current from the battery which is now fastened to the head with rivets.

Doctor Rhubarb's Corner

Question: My nephew lives in a box and wants to be a pelican on a tin stool, but his chest is full of holes and he can't swallow corned beef. My dad rubs his gums with charcoal dropping and his dream is to blow sugar up a Russian's knickers. Everybody likes him and he does a lot for geese.

Answer: Put a prune in a scarf and place it on a bed of toffee. Hold his nose with pliers and fold his feet in well-lit starched pith helmet. Tell him he looks like a submarine."

Les featured on the front cover of Blackpool's summer What's On magazine in June 1984.

Historic Lancashire

Fumble's Folly: Go to Great Eccleston, turn round and back into Wainwright's Copse. Directly ahead you will see the slate heap where Druids used to fry crab's ears as a sacrifice to the God, Arthur.

The folly, circa 1543, is built with balsa wood and mole manure, and many historians believe that the rotunda holds the future of the Liberal Party.

Who Fumble was, nobody knows but legend has it that he led a party of bookmakers into a bog and then ran off with an accountant.

Cream teas are served during the season and small children must take their shoes off in the alcove where the skins are dried.

the
Dawson
Slant

11 November 1982

Last night, as the sun bled its dying warmth over the sewage filter beds, a middle-aged skin specialist with property in Uganda, was dragged into Fairhaven Lake by that vile aquatic abomination who haunts the scowling water… yes, my friends… the Fairhaven Lake Monster strikes again. Thanks to the quick reflexes of a karate instructor from Mothercare, the skin specialist was saved from the jaws of the foul creature with only the loss of a foot and his blazer. For months I have warned the authorities about this menace: all in vain, officialdom still buries its head in the sand bucket. Hackthorn Crumpet, the noted marine biologist, was at my side last Bank Holiday Monday when the grotesque serpent rose to the surface and broke wind. Hackthorn immediately identified the monster, as a "Rectumiunm Piscatosos." Long thought extinct, the serpent is capable of throttling a horse in full flight. Once again, the strip club owners in Ansdell refuse to heed my words, and that seamy, garish district of all-night casinos and wine bars carries on its trade in the pleasures of the flesh.

———————————

A spiritualist who contacted Cromwell's mother during a seance in Hull was attacked by an orphan with measles. Nobody knows why the fool did it, and the police are keeping an open mind about it. "He's done it before," said a man who once shook hands with a ghost, and a lady who can grow a beard under a trance told our reporter that a demon was in her coal shed. Personally, living as I do in St. Annes, I don't believe in the after life, I'd settle for some life here, by George.

———————————

A man who sold lighthouse spares went into liquidation today. He said: "Oldham isn't the place for that sort of thing."

FOR SALE

Oatmeal model of a humped owl with a boil. Made in Munich by Otto Clott, it smells when a bell rings.

Warner Brothers are to make a film on the life of Hetty Gumm, the woman who once hypnotised Hitler with a paint brush. Miss Gumm, who fell off a giraffe in the Orkneys during the Boer war, served in the French Foreign Legion as a trombonist and lived with a Riff in a bakery. Hetty Gumm was an all-round sportswoman who could play golf with a banana. For a time she kept hens in her underskirt and she wrote the Lord's Prayer on the head of a dung beetle. Des O'Conner will play the part of Miss Gumm in her later years as a bus driver and Kirk Douglas will play the cleft in her chin.

Great news for all country and western music fans! Korky Gas and his Tennessee Cocoa Pancakes are to appear in Britain. This sensational band, who play back to front, have just released their latest album, Wheat, Worm Mamma On A Battered Waffle. Great tracks, oh boy, oh boy… out of sight man… yeah.

Policemen have finally captured the South Shore boarding house proprietor, Mrs Wretch, and she is now in custody. Over a number of years, this infamous jade has slaughtered more than 200 holidaymakers who dared ask for extra helpings, and more slayings might well be discovered. A pale detective told me there are fears that a large metal trunk in the garage may well contain the corpses of a Wigan formation dancing team who stayed at the boarding house a month ago. Apparently Mrs Wretch chased some of the dancers with a javelin after one of them had taken a peach off the sideboard.

Lancashire Dishes

Waxed Pony Broth

Take one Exmoor pony that has first been hung in a wire hanger and daub it with turps. Roll it in bacon fat and dry with a flannel. Pour hot wax over the pony and stick its knees in an overcoat. Add grated olives and make a sandwich of the juice and eat it whilst you put almonds in the gravy. Boil for a week with the door open, and never bend down with the lights on. Thread lentils with dried prawn whiskers and serve carefully on a plank.

Les with the Mayor of Blackpool, John Lander, at the switch-on of the Illuminations in 1986.

The pot gnome factory is in the news again. The AUD (short for Associated Union of Dwarfs) is calling for a general strike in order to show the Government that the dwarfs who model for the pixies and garden elves, are grossly underpaid. Speaking from under a chair, the secretary of the AUD, Mr Sam Winkle, told our intrepid reporter that the wage scale for the little people is an insult. "We may be small," he thundered. "But we do have our dignity." It apparently takes over an hour to pose for a polythene imp and Mr Winkle wants cramp money paid to those of his members who crouch with a fishing road. Some dwarfs who specialise in elfin postures, complain of backache and dropsy after leaping from a plastic boulder. Mrs Peppe, who models for trolls and fairies now has to wear a surgical appliance after an incident when she fell on her wand. The Yorkshire miners are to march on Downing Street carrying a midget in a red hat.

Roscoe Chip, who is on trial for blowing eggs through his vest in Preston, tried to escape today disguised as a nun in a convent flute band. He was overpowered by the large woman who claims to be the real Prince Philip, and she smacked his legs with a telescope. Chip is now under maximum security after trying to eat his Action Man.

---

the Dawson Slant

18 November 1982

Thumbs up from Les in September 1988 after a health scare which forced him to quit his summer show at the Opera House.

"Big Moose" Molloy, the Ansdell racketeer who bootlegs bathtub brandy from his distillery behind the Old Bank Tea Shop, was shot in a gunfight last night. Police believe the gunman, who was wearing a rubber mouse mask, is the notorious "Bugsy" Speigel, the Freckleton mobster and lapsed Methodist. Gang warfare in Ansdell is on the increase since my expose of the Fairhaven Lake Monster. Some of the gangsters want to exploit the monster to encourage gamblers to the hot spots; other hoodlums think it will frighten the good-time gals away. I couldn't care less myself, I only play Cluedo.

———————————————

The Rossall Clock Mine has been closed after a miner staggered out with a pendulum round his neck. It seems there was a fall of wrist watches down number four shaft and it pinned a parrot to a wheelbarrow.

Bunkered! Playing from s...
serious stuff for natty dre...
Les in September 1986.

Places to Visit in Lancashire

For a really off-beat holiday, strongly recommended is Miresa On The Crouch. This tiny resort lies about 15 miles from Heysham and is famous for its hunched mussels. It is quite delightful to walk from the old minefield to the wartime barbed wire warehouse, and to stop and view the graveyard where the plague victims are buried. On the jetty, there is an accordion band and a Dutch clairvoyant who gives lectures on amputations. The Hotel

Splendide is closed, but accommodation can be found in a renovated pill box. Hanging Hall is open to the public and for a mere 50p, you can see the remains of Lord Pudding swinging from the gibbet. If you enjoy the smell of rotting halibut, you will love the fish market which lies at the back of a Tudor crypt. Legend has it that every May Day, someone gets into the burial chamber and applauds loudly for an hour, then disappears ... it's known locally as "Who crept in the crypt and clapped and crept out again?"

Has Mankind's meddling with nature gone too far? I have a very reliable report on my desk that a maiden lady with an impeccable background was attacked in a restaurant by a kipper. It went for her throat and it took the combined weight and strength of three Armenian waiters to get the kipper subdued. Two months ago in Wolverhampton a man was severely mauled by a plate of outraged whitebait, and on a golf course recently, a mixed foursome found themselves under attack from a one-eyed rabbit looking for sex.

Personals

Will Bendy Philips, the Wakefield contortionist contact his dad who's sat on a bus with a bag of nuts? Auntie Mary wants her boxer shorts back from him as her purse, made from a cow's shin, is in the back pocket. Thank you.

Swiss-born, Blackpool-based scientist Doctor Helmut Clack, who invented electric braces for people with tall knees, announced that he is in line for the Nobel Prize, and frankly it's not before time, by Jove. This great man has given so much to the world. His achievements are a sonnet to endeavour... 1943: He invented a substance that rots collars. The stuff was rubbed on to the uniforms of a Panzer division and they couldn't wear ties. This caused a lack of morale as well as an outbreak of warts. 1953: He invented gas-fired sandals for people with flat feet and, in the same year, he proved that onions could lip read.

Q&A

Q What is the first thing that attracts you to a member of the opposite sex?

A When they say 'yes'.

Q What do you dislike most about your appearance?

A When they say 'no'.

Q When were/are you happiest?

A That halcyon moment before the first sip.

Q On what occasions, if any, do you lie?

A Never! I'm stood up to the last.

"Cuddles" Gaylord, the international hair stylist from Barnsley, held a showing of his latest creations yesterday. He stunned the assembly of fashion–conscious debutantes with his new "Bald" look for long-haired women. The hair is scrubbed off one side of the head and panel pins are welded to the scalp, then glitter dust is blown over them. Down the other side of the cranium, the hair is cropped and burnt with joss sticks until the skin is blackened and puckered, then a mouse is sewn by the foot to the ear lobe. If this wasn't sensational enough, his favourite model. Desiree, whose mother was Mrs Ginsberg from Ealing, appeared with barbed wire curlers and a wine rack roped to the head and shoulders.

The trial of Mrs Wretch, the South Shore boarding house keeper commenced today with the swearing in of the jury. Mrs Wretch swore at all of them and had to be manacled. This dreadful woman is accused of more than 200 murders at her boarding house, all the victims holidaymakers who had asked for more food. One poor chap clung to her stout brogues and pleaded with Mrs Wretch to tell him what had happened to his sister Agnes from Salop, who had stayed at the house in 1953. The powerfully-muscled barridan butted him on the nose and was heard to snarl: "Agnes, hey? She pinched an extra slice of Angel Cake off my centre table tray… but she never stole anything else mate. She finished up with him who wanted brown bread… I hope they are happy together in the linen chest." Later, it was verified that two skeletons with pike staffs driven through their necks had been found in the said linen chest.

---

the Dawson Slant

25 November 1982

Back to the beach - Les in knotted hanky during filming of the TV programme *A Century of Stars* in 1985.

Les said in September 1990: "If you don't smoke or drink, what do you do? You die healthy that's what! I'd rather end up in a box and have people think that at least I had a good time while I was here."

Dad in waiting – Les with an expectant Tracy in February 1992.

Historic Lancashire

Clump House: Built as a Tudor bungalow, this seven-storey dwelling, designed by De Vere of Runcorn, is a masterpiece of simplicity. Upstairs, in the great cellar, is a fine example of a stone coffin that was used to cement syrup in.

Old Duke Hicks, who lost his memory in a volcano, lived there for some time until his boil was lanced.

During the Georgian period, an attic was put under the floorboards and Morris dancers went there to have a shave. Legend says that a Boer fireman went damp in a tea chest once, and Miss Hubbcapp, who chases parked cars, said that for years no pancake would bounce on the landing.

A keen gardener, whose wife was shoved in a Venus Fly Trap plant, lost his trousers in a clump of gladioli after a drinking bout with a solicitor. This is yet another incident in the growing disgrace of gardening orgies. A masked cadet had peat smeared on his suspenders by a caped nude in a thicket recently, and a missing landscape architect was found eating things from a bundle with a well–known flower arranger in a potting shed full of blue movies.

A Kendal hermit who last year crossed a giraffe with a cow today announced that he had a six foot chop for sale. A butcher sneered at the news and said it was daft. The hermit (nobody knows his name) speaks with a Bulgarian accent and can play a tune on a shovel. For years the Kendal authorities have tried to get rid of him by throwing money up his skirt, but he just runs into the Town Hall and waxes the mayor's legs.

A couple who claim they escaped from Silas Grimmly's holiday camp in Wolverhampton disguised as dog handlers, are to be placed under police protection pending further investigation into the goings on at the holiday centre. The couple, who were interviewed by me, insisted on complete anonymity, and were dressed in Donald Duck costumes. They talked of being beaten up by the camp comic and forced to do a quickstep for refusing an egg custard. Apparently, no camper could dodge the mass swim to the Orkneys and paper hats and red noses were compulsory. A man from Swindon who tried to dig a tunnel out of the camp was thrown to a moray eel and his wife and son were nailed by the foot to a plank whilst the commandant played a Jimmy Shand record.

Last night on stage at the Freckleton Opera House, Madam Gerta Bugri set fire to her pullover with a faulty Dunhill after a row with a Mormon who exposed his backside to a woman who claims she is the real Prince Philip. Madam Gerta received a standing ovation when she fried his jock strap in a charcoal bag after singing Lily Of Laguna.

Marvin Looe, who does a lot for charity attempted to swim the channel last week with a harp on his back. He reported high winds after he had landed on the beach at Norway.

Doctor Rhubarb's Corner

Question: After drinking a canal dry, my wife complained of a swelling on her braces when she smoked a side of bacon up a trapeze. Now she's started to ask if she can put a window in the cat, and gets very angry when she can't bend salmon. I've tried rolling logs on her chest when she spits at geese with dandruff, but all she does is laugh with her truss back to front and tattoos dead bricks with hot ink.

Answer: She's suffering from backswill of the knee with acute signs of pickles acne. Put her in a parcel of mice and let her tap dance on a domino. Keep her away from two –storey spin driers and let her sing in the oven.

the Dawson Slant

2 December 1982

Hildegarde Crumm, the sex symbol in Russian movies, has been signed up to appear in Crossroads as a steamboat captain with a bad heart. Miss Crumm, who was formerly the wife of Ivan Ivanovitch, the Moscow specialist in bed wetting, said today she was delighted to be in this country and wanted to see up a Gordon Highlander's kilt. Miss Crumm's greatest role was in the film Hunchback of Notre Dame. She was the hump up Charlie Laughton's back and won an Oscar for being able to hang from his braces.

The FBI are to be called in to quell the gang war that is raging in Ansdell. Not only are we plagued with such number one enemies as: "Moose" Molloy, "Fingers" McCoy and "Killer" Garciano, now "Lefty" Kowasky has joined forces with Harry (The Horse) Jones. It also seems the strip joints and flash nightclubs and casinos will bring into the conflict "Dutch" Shultz, "Bullets" Moran and "Machine Gun" Kelly. I only hope "Legs" Moran and "Diamond" Jacobski don't team up with "Bugsy" Speigel and "Daggers" Marciano. Boom Boom La Tour, a blonde nude and personal friend on Friday afternoons, told me in private that a short broad with pink eyes took a shot at "Tigers" Moffat in the Rummy Room of the Ansdell all-male strip revue. He managed to wing "Fats" Riley before "Nick the Greek" Johson got him.

Les was never short of a bright idea!

Latest fashion news from that zingy designer, Bo Bo Wimpey! His autumn collection, darlings, is a must for all bright Young Things.....A trailing gown with a handkerchief hem, sets off with a sparkle the flounced organdie strapless donkey jacket in burnt sienna....Hip-length gaiters with rubber panels give an allure to the string vest and pleated nose rope....And for those slumbering summer nights...a see-through pair of weighted socks and carnival cap in blue serge.

An upholsterer who pierces ears while you wait, claimed his wife was the original model for Space Invaders and is demanding money from seaside amusement arcades. He wouldn't meet me face to face and i had to talk to him through a cushion.

He freely admitted he lied about his cat having shingles and said some rotten things about Mussolini.

Les pictured at The Grand Theatre, Blackpool, in September 1988.

More news of unemployment. The last North Sea curry pump station closed today and 16 men with long necks, who used to suck the stuff up through starched tubes, have been made redundant. So much money has been lost on this ill-fated venture that the very senses reel in impotent fury at realisation that the tasty vindaloo gleaned from the seabed will no longer get this country out of its present mess. In a moving ceremony this morning in Barrow, the last mouthful was spat into a brass pot and then buried in the floor of a building society. In India, of course, there was great rejoicing at the news and a hooligan took off his loincloth and streaked through a missionary's bathroom.

A violinist who taught his trousers to sing the National Anthem is to go on television to show viewers how to teach an orange to yodel. Des O'Connor will do a duet with the fruit and if it's successful, there will be a series featuring a set of twins who gargle with canaries and a lapsed weightwatcher who hatches out carrots under his armpit.

A football match was interrupted on Saturday when a dwarf wearing nothing but cardboard shorts, jumped into the referee's shirt and bit his Adam's apple. This is yet another grave incident in the spiralling crisis of the Pot Gnome Strikers. Everywhere, dwarfs are showing their anger at the

Do-it-yourself Corner

This week: How to make a set of woollen eyebrows.

Superb relaxation for the winter months. Knit a short row on a flat copper needle and chew until moist. Fluff out the ends of the wool, which should be still attached to the sheep. Lie sideways in a coma and glue your lip to a pole. Cross-weave the wool if the sheep's blouse comes off and give it some All-Bran. Place on head and edge the smooth side down the forehead proper until the eyes meet in the middle. Walk to one side and put milk in a wig.

Government's reluctance to give them cramp money, free shaves and low pedestals in public conveniences. The dwarfs spend hours posing in various postures as imps, goblins and good old fashioned elves, but it can play havoc with their prostate glands and in some cases, they catch dandruff of the knee.

A red parrot with yellow lumps on its six-foot beak was seen today on the M62 by Rollo Stump the well known ornithologist and town drunk.

the Dawson Slant

9 December 1982

A meat pie that can tell the time by doing cartwheels was stolen from the home of Miss Vanessa Pulp, the celebrated buffalo hoof designer and female liberationist, whose book- "How to Clone Elephants for Profit" is a best-seller in Acton. Miss Pulp discovered the theft when she returned from a picnic held in a Nuneaton octopus farm. Miss Pulp, who is 73 but looks shorter, lived for a while in Uganda but didn't like it.

———————————————

More fashion news for the ladies! Bo Bo Wimpey, the darling boy let a few selected friends see his latest breathtaking collection of beach water for those simply super hols. Firstly we saw his quite mad copper-tipped bikini in bright puce, with a tin-embroidered hem peeping from the gusset. Then, sweeties, on came his divine two-piece-backless off-the-hips self-draining swimsuit that gives a new dimension to pigeon chests. A towelling robe goes with the two-piece and that is a sonnet in flounced leather and slate pegs.

———————————————

The Pot Gnome Strike grows and soon the army may be used to stop the dwarfs who model for the gnomes and pixies from putting rude sayings up on the walls of houses where tall people live. The TUC declared their support for the dwarfs and engineers in Luton have welded their ears to a Vauxhall saloon in sympathy. Meanwhile, a consignment of clay imps and coy fairies on turtles have been sprayed with ointment in a warehouse. An MP who found a male dwarf in his haversack had to be treated for shock at a clinic after the midget had given him a set of black knees.

———————————————

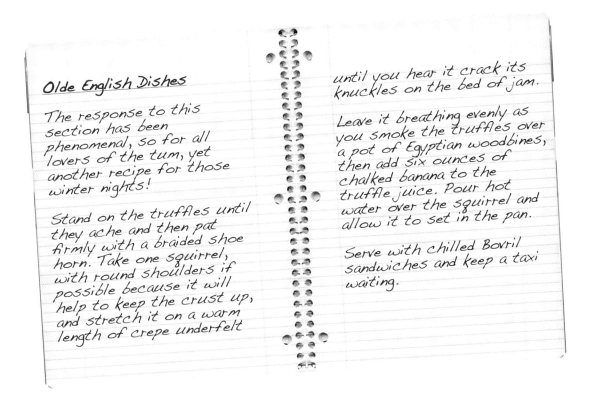

Olde English Dishes

The response to this section has been phenomenal, so for all lovers of the tum, yet another recipe for those winter nights!

Stand on the truffles until they ache and then pat firmly with a braided shoe horn. Take one squirrel, with round shoulders if possible because it will help to keep the crust up, and stretch it on a warm length of crepe underfelt until you hear it crack its knuckles on the bed of jam.

Leave it breathing evenly as you smoke the truffles over a pot of Egyptian woodbines, then add six ounces of chalked banana to the truffle juice. Pour hot water over the squirrel and allow it to set in the pan.

Serve with chilled Bovril sandwiches and keep a taxi waiting.

A Defence spokesman said yesterday that the Russians have perfected a new and deadly weapon; a brace-rotting gas. Any regiment attacking a Russian position would be sprayed with the gas and soldiers would not be able to keep their trousers up.
A purple Whitehall brigadier said: "Infernal Russkis, this could change the whole face of conventional war, damn it." Swiss-born Blackpool-based scientist Doctor Helmut Clack is said to be working on a pair of underpants that will unfurl into overalls once the gas rots through the braces.

Hildergarde Crumm, the russian sex symbol has admitted having an affair with an Italian joiner. Miss Crumm, over here to play in Crossroads, was unrepentant about her stormy love association with a man 26 years her junior. Miss Crumm, who plays the part of a steamboat captain with a bad heart, said she intends to divorce her husband Ivan Ivanovitch, the bed-wetting specialist, because he's started doing it.

That straight-talking MP Mr Rumpole Woolly talked to me last Friday about nuclear disarmament. "Of course it's a two-edged problem," he boomed. "Either way, this or that, it's a difficult business. As for myself, my views are clear cut... if the bomb is here then that's that, and if it wasn't it would be the same, let me make this quite clear. "The short term is longer than the long term and that's a fact not a definite maybe. We have to consider or think about it a lot in my opinion which isn't only mine if we think about it."

Blackpool's own boxing hero, former British heavyweight champion Brian London, shows Les what a real moustache looks like in March 1986.

"On growing a moustache, Les said: " It was horrible. I hated it. The thing took ages to grow and when it did it was all in clumps and looked like a rancid faggot."

the Dawson Slant

16 December 1982

A Wolverhampton lay preacher with a bad arm who fell into a parcel of turtle manure, claimed today his feet have grown whiskers. I personally believe him, because my nephew, Seymour Offit who was a road manager for a yoga steel band before he walled up his mother in Cromer, had a friend who once wired up a depressed turtle to a gas lamp for Christmas, and afterwards went into a coma when he found lumps of wet hair growing from his lip. A Japanese firm is to market the stuff for the general public, bald or otherwise.

———————————

That straight-talking, no-nonsense politician, Mr Rumpole Woolly is to face critics at the onion workers social club. His view on nuclear energy is a study in common sense. "Energy is energy, what?" He told me yesterday "Whichever way you put it, it's still the same, that's what I say and do, of course, that's why i said it… and i am a man of my word, believe me, that's what I say. What's the point of saying it if what i say doesn't make sense? Of course there is energy, and energy, and if that is true, that's what I'm saying isn't it?"

———————————

The pot gnome strike is attracting more sympathy, and the little men who model for the fish pond figurines are delighted. Arthur Scargill has promised to stop his miners buying clay elves and fairies and the TUC are to hold a dance for the dwarfs in January.

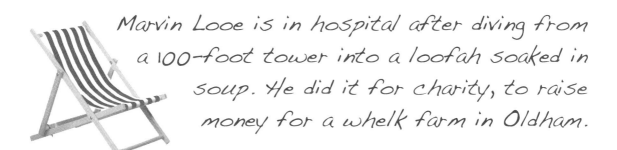

Marvin Looe is in hospital after diving from a 100-foot tower into a loofah soaked in soup. He did it for charity, to raise money for a whelk farm in Oldham.

Swiss-born, Blackpool-based scientist, Dr Helmut Clack, is in trouble again. This time he has angered the Arab world with his sale to them of electrical braces for people with tall knees. It appears that some desert Riffs were found wandering about the Sahara Desert with their trousers three foot above their heads. Salim (of God himself) Mustapha, the man who bought the braces in good faith, told our reporter that the cut-out switches melted under the hot sun and the fan bells under the Riffs' robes snapped after rubbing against the camel humps.

The trial of Mrs Wretch, the South Shore boarding house keeper, is an exercise in Gothic horror. A masked witness told a hushed court that he had escaped from a sea chest that Mrs Wretch had shoved him in after he had asked her for an extra slice of pork luncheon meat. "I was very hungry at the time," he whispered. "Otherwise I would not have asked for it. Mrs Wretch dragged me in the limo and bundled me into the stout leather box and said she was going to throw me in the sea. As I lay there in the darkness, through the keyhole, I saw her load a blunderbuss and I heard her say quite distinctly, "That whining old so and so in number 11 wants another blanket does he? Well it will be his shroud'." A delicate juror fainted and the case was adjourned when Mrs Wretch went for the judge's throat.

Bo Bo Wimpey, the celebrated dress designer, has done it again for you trendies! This time it's off-the-shoulder knickers in crimped tin. A saucy hat with bells on sets off the sturdy pants to perfection, and the trailing length of chewed silk gives a new dimension to the hip. A cross-over bronze cable holds the knickers to the scalp for casual wear, and for those warm nights, two slivers of plywood on the back, help to create the illusion of abandon.

Personals

Please will Bendy Philips, the contortionist whose dad is sat on a bus with a bag of nuts, fetch the purse made out of a cow's chin and give it to Miriam, who's lost an ear in an avalanche.

The woman who claims she is the real Prince Philip took her frock off outside the tattoo parlour in protest against a rates increase. "We've got to do something," she yelled as police scrubbed a rude drawing of Wedgewood Been off her vest.

Les was banking on laughs when he opened a new Natwest service till in St Annes Square in January 1981.

"It won't affect me too much. I have no money to draw out", quipped Les. " Everytime I come to this bank the manager waves me off with his red cloth-it's an overdraft excluder"

the **Dawson Slant**

24 December 1982

Once again, dear, dear reader, it's Christmas… you can always tell when it's Christmas, Easter eggs are in the shops. Personally I don't like the Festive Season, religion's creeping into it. Mind you for many years I was an atheist…but I gave it up when I found I wasn't getting any holidays.

When I was a mere child, Christmas was a time of hardship. I never had any toys, except for a Do-It-Yourself electric train set that dad gave me one year… It turned out to be a roll of fuse wire and a platform ticket.

Of course I came from a big family, and on Christmas Day it was five-a-side to a cracker. The dinner was always the same… Peruvian woodcock; in fact it was a black pudding with a feather stuck in it. The whole family went to church on Christmas Day morning; mother used to mug off the sidesman for the coins on the plate and dad stole the lead off the roof, I was too young to mug the vicar so my sister did it with an axe. The following year we lost dad, he didn't die, we just lost him.

Freckleton royal opera is to stage a Jewish pantomime called Abe's In The Wood. Madam Gerti Bugri will sing the hit song: I did it oy vay. A large cast has been assembled. Poulton's very own massed piano marching band will play Jingle Bells in the foyer and Morrison's jumping infants will geld a mongoose for charity.

There ain't nothing like a dame! Les as Ada the Cook in *Dick Whittington* at the Manchester Palace Theatre in September 1990.

Les with Ray Cornell's dancers during rehearsals for his Grand Theatre summer show in June 1984.

The woman who claims she is the real Prince Philip told an orphan under a quilt last night that she did in fact have an affair with Father Christmas in a Co-op grotto. The orphan, aged 42, sobbed openly when she shoved mistletoe up his vest and tried to kiss his braces. A store detective who had his teeth glued to a box of Lego escorted the woman out and let her autograph his mother.

A turkey that stands on its beak and recites the Gettysburg Address was inadvertently plucked and stuffed last night in readiness for eating. The woman who did it said: "It never said a bloody word to me."

There will be no Christmas cheer in Garstang. The Russian caviar salesman have banned all dancing in the pubs and the only song allowed will be the Volga Boatman. I think it is rotten the way these damned sales reps are allowed to flaunt their product in a Lancashire town, but the fishy stuff is catching on and the sale of pig's trotters is down.

———————————

A Ghost Story For Christmas

The snowflakes, incensed by a maddened wind, blew a white blanket across the stark branches of the old oak tree. Nearby, as the clock struck twelve, a red setter without a tail, knocked on the door of a lonely inn. The landlady opened the door and the dog said: "When I was alive, you cut my tail off... I want it back." The woman said softly: "I'm sorry, Rover, we cant re-tail spirits after 10:30."

———————————

May I wish my readers a very merry Christmas, and in the words of Alf Chopp, the Burnley poet: "Drink a cup if there is one or not, should a cork be rammed up a ferret's cap, will it no droop the hem of a matador's knickers?"

Doctor Rhubarb's Corner

Question: When my husband hangs his stocking up, he ties it tightly around my neck. He does this after hiding mince pies on the top of a burnt rafter. Since he lost his ankle in a raffle, he tends to get moody and spin dry herrings in a paper hat. He spoils Christmas by whistling in the oven and he's wallpapered the Labrador and throws pickles at a Dutchman. Should I keep him in hot trousers or let him get sentimental over old-fashioned elbows?

Answer: Your husband is going through a period of adjustment. This happens when mice run down his sleeve. Keep him in a spare bungalow with a pan of rivets and swill his wig with steamed gin every time his shirt lap catches fire.

The Fairhaven Lake monster was sighted yesterday morning by a Mr Kelvin Boote, a master plumber who busks on a flute in Ansdell. He told a friend of his, who wears a frock on alternative Mondays, that he heard it break wind as it rose to the surface for a scratch. Mr Boote isn't a very reliable person, he once accused Dolly Parton of shoving egg boxes up her blouse. However, there is some evidence to suggest that the monster doesn't exist. I have heard it said that when my wife fell in Fairhaven water, the monster got out and picketed the lake.

It is written in the Lost Book of the Old Ones that the world will end in Preston. I received this startling information from an Hungarian chef who can foresee the future… from up a newt's colon. When I suggested that his was a most unorthodox method, he forcible shaved my legs and told me I had a twin living in Knutsford. Actually I haven't got a twin but I do have a sister in Tobruck who won't admit the war's over.

Doctor Armitage Bunkle allowed me to interview him the other day. Readers of the Lancet will, of course, know that Dr Bunkle is the man who claims to have invented a pill that retards age. The venerable Dr Bunkle is well over 93 and looks every inch of it, but after taking one pill, he sat on the settee and before my eyes his voice changed to that of a younger man and within an hour he started to cry and said he wanted to poo. The only trouble with the pill is he still looked well over 93 in his romper suit.

---

the Dawson Slant

30 December 1982

There is something terribly wrong with Garstang. I have information on my desk that would seem to indicate the Russians are taking over the pubs in the town. Ever since they tried for home rule, the inhabitants of Garstang have been bothered by fringe lunatics and Liberals who've lost their deposits. Now it appears as if the Russian paratroops who landed in the town a week ago, are not soldiers at all but caviar salesman, and if a respectable toper goes in a pub to get loaded, he's not allowed a drink until he's bought three ounces of Black Sea Caviar first. I find this intolerable and I can't stand the stuff. I know something of the Russian mentality. I toured Siberia some years ago, I was only there a week… it should have been a longer stay, but I had trouble with the language, because in Russia everything ends in "Off!"

———————————————

For all lovers of "hard rock" music, in town next week is Suggy Mukk and the Asteroids. This band, who recorded in a chest freezer, are currently touring shoe shops in Harwich, and business is so good, Freeman and Hardy are stood on Willis. On lead gas pipe is Jay Jay Cooe, and on the manhole lid is Ossy Croke. It's a great sound – to hear it through a wall of lettuce is an experience.

———————————————

He's at it again! Marvin Looe, who does a lot for charity, is to attempt to sellotape mussels up his wife's back whilst being rolled down the M62 in a bin full of flour. He's doing this for an adult orphans who can't tell the time in bed. Marvin's a great guy and I personally wish him well, although frankly he's a bit daft sometimes.

———————————————

A new game for all the family is on sale now. Called "Grope" it is fun for all ages. Simply, all one has to do is roll a round dice up a person's socks and the first one to shout "Gobble" takes a handful of dandruff and crams it in a wet underskirt. If the answer is no the next player stands with his back to the traffic and counts up to a million while the other players wallpaper their feet.

———————————————

The German who can hypnotise bricks has done it again… last night he made the St Annes Town Hall doze off for 15 minutes, but it didn't create much interest really, because nobody noticed the difference. Meanwhile I can't find anybody to pay my rates.

the Dawson Slant

7 January 1983

In this, a new series on great Britons, I would like to commence by eulogising an Englishman who, I am sorry to say, passed away a few months ago. His name was D. D. Titbitt. Apparently he drank a small firkin of malt whiskey and died of a new disease… ecstasy. Rumour has it that three weeks after he was buried you could still smell his breath at the inquest. His wife said yesterday: "The only plants that grow on his grave are hops." Titbitt was such a heavy drinker, his birth certificate was written on a cork. On one occasion, he was five minutes late for opening time and brewery shares slumped. Titbitt was a little chap and every time he pulled his underpants up, he blindfolded himself. He was so small he suffered from athlete's foot on his chin. His father was a weaver who accidentally fell in a loom and warped his weft, and when he was finally laid to rest, everybody looked up to him, because he was buried in a tree. It was in 1932 that Titbitt stumbled across a case of gin and he went on stumbling for the next six months. His nose was so red he was hired to warn in shipping in the Mersey. He was alas, most anaemic, in fact when he was pulled up for the breathalyser test the policeman had to give him a blood transfusion before he could take a sample. When he went abroad, he drank so much alcohol, his wife had to pay duty on him at customs. Neighbours said there were so many empty bottles in Titbitt's garden, it put £300 on the price of the house. He's gone now, and missed by many of us, but his philosophy will never be forgotten. "A friend in need… is a pest."

Les on the Blackpool sands with fellow comedian Frank Carson in May 1988.

Newly-crowned King of Lights Les meets his Queen, Karel Horton, in July 1985.

Good news for all holidaymakers! Whoop's Tours have announced a new coach trip from Oldham to Tibet. Commencing next May, the trip will take a year and all passengers can take out buttock cramp insurance at Knutsford. The new coaches will have swimming pools and video films, PLUS a saucy massage parlour and late night cabaret. This is despite the failure of Whoop's continental tour of 16 countries in three days, when passengers suffered nose bleeds and loss of gravity in Holland. One lady who survived the trip told me that the coach went through Italy so fast, when she took a photograph of Rome, all she got was a smell of garlic and a vapour trail.

The pot gnome strike drew further support today from 33 members of the TMC (Truss Mechanics Confederation). Their spokesman Harry Crabbstone said: "We in the Truss business know all about giving someone full support, and I can promise you there will be hold-ups with our appliances." Meanwhile, a dwarf who poses for clay-fired rockery pixies was arrested outside Downing Street for hiding in Maggie Thatcher's handbag.

There was another ugly shoot-out in the Old Bank Tea Shoppe last night. Al "Big Nose" Bunion peppered "Busy" Siegel with air gun pellets, and "Hoots" Carter, along with "Moose" Molloy, hit the dirt. Ansdell is now the crime centre of the western world, and the growing number of strip clubs, casinos, illicit stills and good time girls in only serving to inflame the situation. Add to that the menace of the Fairhaven Lake Monster, who is eating everybody in

Book Review

My Life in a Tin by Clement Froo. A poignant tale of skin grafting in Malaya. Mr Froo, who built a Liberal Club with mongoose droppings and old corsets, tells of his struggles to learn Hebrew inside a box. For many years he smoked strips of halibut in bed and lost his uncle down a bottle. Chapter five is colourful; it's in red chalk, and smells of cheese. For many readers, his description of an iced loincloth hanging from a catapult, will be the nub of the novel. Mr Froo, who is on a pension, has written 97 books without the use of a pen and his feet are his own. Priced at £10 a square inch, the book is a fine investment, and a reminder of the great days of bandana bending in Rangoon. I liked it, and still do, thanks to ginseng.

sight – a cassock has been found in a clump of groundsel – and you have an explosive problem. Even ordinary tradesmen are adopting the gangster-type nicknames… Kelly (Newsagents) "The Ink" Newsagents and Booths "The Chew Chew" superstore. Even my wife is affected by it, and now calls herself "Nags" Dawson.

"The girl was so thin her husband used her as a spirit level. She overdosed on Alka Seltzer and fizzed to death."

The Pentagon, in answer to the Russians' latest weapon – a gas which rots braces – have engaged a leading European concern to further a series of experiments on an explosive that can blow up army socks. In this country, Swiss-born, Blackpool-based scientist, Doctor Helmut Clack, is still going ahead with his expanding vest theory. The idea is that should the Russians use their gas, and should it indeed rot our troops' braces whilst charging say, a pillbox, the fact that their trousers would fall down would not cause confusion because the vest would unfurl and cover vital areas. The French, as usual, are going their own way by sending their soldiers in with nothing on at all. This, they say, will keep costs down and enable them to peg council house rents.

The new leader of the Manure Baggers Union, Dennis Acorn, is a left wing right of centre, politically-speaking. He narrowly defeated Max Clocke, who is right wing with leftish tendencies, but liberal in some ways. This is a big victory for left wing moderates and right wing communists who are fighting off middle-of-centre left wing fascists who support middle-of-the-road extremists with big noses. Anyone for tennis?

The Fairhaven Lake Monster is an amphibious reptile and that is a fact. Last night the repugnant creature broke into a jeweller's caravan and ate a Yorkshire terrier. Will somebody do something about this? Otherwise nobody will be safe in their beds. Why, even my own wife could become a victim. Wait a minute lads, on second thoughts let's not do anything too hasty. We certainly live in a wonderful world. Following my recent story last week about

the Dawson Slant

13 January 1983

Miss Vanessa Pulp and her meat pie that could tell the time by doing cartwheels, a gentleman from Cheltenham wrote and loftily informed me that he once trained a Cornish pasty to recite the Gettysburg Address whilst hanging from a joist. Its name was Arthur and it was a very jolly sort and never bit the kids. Alas it contracted rabies in Glossop and flaked to death.

There was a dramatic incident during the trial of Mrs Wretch, the landlady of the South Shore boarding house, who is accused of slaughtering any holidaymaker who asked for more. A roll of carpet was dragged into court, and when it was unfurled, out popped the corpse of a man dressed in shorts, and wearing a "Kiss-Me-Quick" cardboard trilby. He was identified as William Glimpsod who has been missing ever since he asked Mrs Wretch for an extra strand of watercress. Apparently he had been beaten to death with a leg of mutton and submerged in Guinness. Mrs Wretch blew a raspberry at the council for the prosecution and carried on bending a bugle.

Marvin Looe, who does a lot for charity, is to carry a cow on his hop down the M1 in order to raise money to send out-of-work Zulus to Florida for a week's motorbike scramble. Marvin, who for years was a caddy on a golf driving range, came to national attention when he successfully held his breath under a Turkish wrestler's armpit to raise funds to buy second hand Jewish bagels for a harpist who had fallen down a lift shaft.

A set of dentures made out of Hungarian onyx with tungsten-tipped molars was found in a tin of treacle on the beach at Dunkirk. Inside the bottom half are the words: "To Daphne with love always, Alf." A Chelsea pensioner with sore gums denied they were his and nastily sucked our reporter's elbow during a Scrabble session.

Doctor Rhubarb's Corner

Question: Ever since my son lost his neck in a disco his feet give off a blue smoke. He used to like carrots dipped in gravy off a pig's lip but now he just locks himself in his singlet and arm wrestles with a whelk. His daddy gave him a rubber rate to chew, but it melted in a mitten and we're full of flies. Can anything be done to get him jumping again?

Answer: Ticklish problem especially in brown paper if the lights are on. Try nailing the singlet to a baked horse and shove the whelk in a casserole every Thursday morning until its shoes let rain in. Don't limp on a serviette unless a bus is due and smear his cap with corn oil.

A group of cubs took a shine to Les during the recording of a radio programme in May 1984.

Q&A

Q What is your biggest regret?

A Never having seen an owl mate.

Q If you could choose another career, what would it be?

A A shepherd in Lambeth.

Q Do you believe in God?

A What's more important - does God believe in me.

Q Would you like to live again?

A Only if there's a radical change in pub prices.

the Dawson Slant

20 January 1983

I recently went to place a sprig of wild hyacinth on the grass knoll that marks the last resting place of Wimberry Hoot, the Blackburn songwriter, who is now forgotten. He would have been the world's greatest songwriter and composer, but for one major physical defect… he was colour blind. Remember those songs of his that so nearly became famous?

"I want Some Green Roses For A Red Lady"

"Puce Sails in the Sunset"

"Brown Moon"

"A Grey Sports Coat and a Black Carnation." What a shame!

The Pot gnome strike is bringing the country to its knees and now violence rears its ugly head. Last night, in a laundrette, three dwarfs locked themselves in a spindryer and wouldn't come out. The dwarfs, who model for garden gnomes and elves, are demanding cramp money and free shaves, but the Government is determined not to give in. The spokesman for the little chaps, Mr Sam Winkle, talked to me today from underneath an alabaster mushroom and kicked my shin. In London, two dwarfs are sitting on top of Nelson's column and the only thing that could get them down in a hurry are the pigeons. The authorities are feeding them Trill mixed with prune juice.

Clown Harry's joke shop was robbed yesterday. The intruder stole 500 knitted freckles, 16 cardboard running noses, two parcels of three dimensional pimples that water, ten false humps and a werewolf's foot. Clown Harry told me that it had taken him years to stock such impish delights, and then sold me an inflatable kneecap.

In Town This Week

Martha Haggett's Trombone Romany Band and Cissie Jelly, the female soot juggler and tree impressionist.

A capacity crowd at the Liver Clinic and Thermal Baths gave a warm reception to Horace Johnson, the one-legged tightrope walker, whose speciality is falling off. Horace, aged 81, can eat a meat pie under hot mud and is still capable of shooting the eyebrow off a salmon. His wife, Mona, sings upside down in a kettle with her elbows tied to a brick fireplace. They don't make acts like that anymore, hey?

The trial of Mrs Wretch, the South Shore boarding house keeper and mass murderer is to be staged next month, and it already promises to be the sensation of the century. To represent the Crown: Sir Hoagfudge Baghott-Babble. The defence of Mrs Wretch is in the hands of Sir Mainwaring Chuff-Wallbanger, the able barrister who successfully defended a man who married a horse during the war. Meanwhile more atrocities are coming to light at the grisly boardinghouse. A charred corpse was found in a microwave oven and identified as Albert Armhole, a holiday-maker from Durham, who asked Mrs Wretch for an extra spoonful of mint sauce. An eyewitness, wearing a bag over her head to avoid recognition, told a hushed assembly of newspapermen, that Mrs Wretch hit Albert with a bucket of fruit, then skinned him alive. Police have also unearthed the body of a young lady wrapped in newspaper. The victim had been clubbed with a battery-driven tin opener. When faced with the remains, Mrs Wretch snarled: "That strumpet, she got what was coming to her… she dared ask me for two extra slices of malt bread." We've just heard that another body has been unearthed from the trunk in the attic, with a stale bun rammed down the victim's throat.

Last night at the Freckleton Royal Opera House, during the jousting scene from the opera Swill It Up Lads – a contemporary work - Madam Gerta Bugri lost her pitchfork when the bull moose she was riding gave birth in the orchestra pit. The good lady's corset broke and a whalebone strut took the oboeist's dentures out.

Car enthusiast Les, who loved his E-type convertible, gives a push start to a mini-Jaguar at Dutton Forshaw's *Sixty Years of Jaguar* event in September 1982.

Q&A

Q What do you always carry with you?

A Trousers, hip flask, leg flask, side flask, hat flask.

Q What vehicle do you drive?

A E-type Lada with body kit.

Q Where is your favourite holiday destination?

A Any Highland distillery.

Q Which question was hardest to answer in this questionnaire?

A All of them were in-depth thought-provoking gobbets of eruditional couplets - some quite corybantic in essence others open to interpellation, but not in the orbit of mendicancy.

the Dawson Slant

27 January 1983

Well I certainly stirred up a hornet's nest in last week's column when I mentioned Wimberry Hoot, the colour-blind songwriter. (Remember his hit number, The Birth of the Greens?). It seems from readers' letters, that not only was he colour-blind but he was also lousy at geography. In all, Hoot wrote three great novels: North Pacific, All Quiet on the Eastern Front, and last but not least, West of Eden. Another avid reader of this column states that Hool was so cross-eyed, he once went to Cardiff to get a job on the Glasgow buses.

On the subject of ecology, my suggestion that Man has interfered too much with nature, certainly upset the applecart for many people. Writing from Dorset, a noted birdwatcher tells me he's given birdwatching up because the birds are now watching him. A Mr Pilbeam from Harrogate had a most harrowing experience with his son's pet guinea pig. Apparently Mr Pilbeam smacked the rodent for stealing a pork chop, and the creature got him in a half-nelson wrestling hold, and then threw a bottle of Friar's Balsam at him. We have to face facts: the animal world is becoming aggressive towards our constant meddling hence the incident last Tuesday when a sex starved turtle in Brisbane plucked the feathers from a cockerel with intent to commit an indecent act, after it had tried to make love to a German infantryman's helmet.

Championing a good cause – Les in June 1993.

On playing the lead role of non-stop eating grandmother Nona in a television black comedy, Les reckoned that the BBC offered him the role because they were cutting costs.

"They had to create this horrible character – and with me, they saved a fortune in make up."

Life's a beach, Summer 1984.

A farmer is to sue the St Annes Council after his prize pig was eaten by the Fairhaven Lake Monster. Last night he left the poor animal's trotters on the doorstep of a noted alderman and loudly demanded, as compensation, a flutch of bacon and free parking. Of course, the nightclub gangsters in Ansdell still refuse to admit that there is something quite foul in the lake and the gang war continues: This morning a milkman with a bad foot found "Moose" Molloy and "Killer" Garciano mugging a paper boy who turned out to be "Fingers" McCoy, the racketeer from Woodland Road. "Lefty" Kowasky and his mob are taking over the Old Bank Tea Shop and turning it into a white slave centre, but they'll still serve cream teas and scones.

A Yorkshire iron monger who runs his Morris Minor on refined chicken manure, said today that he gets a lot of pleasure out of his car. "It's a pleasure to get out of it," he added. His wife, who has scars on her nose from using clothes pegs, said she is very lonely: "'E might get 47 miles to the gallon, but we've got no friends." The smell is frankly appalling and twice now his neighbour has blown his tyres off with gelignite. A spokesman for Shell Oil admitted his usage of dung might pose a threat should he ever be able to add aftershave lotion to it, but at present they were content to wait and see.

I talked to that eminent member of Parliament, Mr Rumpole Woolly, yesterday about our current problems and it was refreshing to hear his straight forward views. On the subject of unemployment he maintained it was just an ugly rumour by a lot of people out of work. "You must realise," he boomed, "that the shifting sands

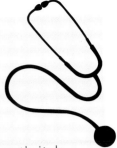

Doctor Rhubarb's Corner

Question: "My husband's teeth itch when he puts his head under gravy and I can't get to him to wear an inner tube on his waistcoat unless there's an "F" in the month. The hair on his thumb is falling out when he wallpapers his tongue at Christmas and my mother's underpants are growing watercress through my husband's use of camel fat on his gannex spats.

Answer: "Your husband should roll his ears in a trough of butter and put a windmill on his hat if his legs are on fire. Hold him by a pulley wheel when he snorts under gravy hum an Al Jolson medley, and send your mother to Bognor."

of economy move in several directions, left or right, but does it matter? Taking a high view or a low view, it will always stay the way it is or remain the way it is. Reading between the lines or over them is a case of principle if you care to understand or not. Either way it is different in one or two instances. The past is gone and the future is yet to come or to put it another way, tomorrow isn't here yet and yesterday went the day before today." Most clear his opinions. I thought or would you rather be a mute?

the Dawson Slant

3 February 1983

There is a strong possibility that Swiss-born, Blackpool-based scientist, Doctor Helmut Clack, will be considered for the Nobel Prize for Peace. This follows the sale of his electric braces for people with tall knees to both Iraq or Iran. From what we can glean, both countries supplied their armed forces with the braces and in the first major battle, the cut-out switches on the leather braces blew up and all the troops involved finished up with their trousers wrapped around their helmets. Several soldiers had their underpants throttled by the flying fan belts, and one sergeant of artillery lost a rotor arm up a delicate region. The battle was stopped while the soldiers sorted their uniforms out. By that time, it had gone dark and it didn't seem worth carrying on.

———————————

A Frenchman who swallowed a bucket was rushed to hospital today and he's not allowed visitors. Why he did it nobody knows, and he hasn't paid for it. The handle of the bucket is stuck on his tonsils and he's having trouble gargling. His knees are his own and they are roughly the same age.

———————————

Garstang is in the news again. Last night, Russian paratroopers were dropped in the wistful town and sang at a wedding reception. General Fog, who led the Home Rule for Garstang fight, had a drink with the Russians and commented that they were a nice bunch of chaps, but spilled a lot. "They'll never get their hands on Gibraltar," said the councillor who's rotten at geography, but nobody seems to know what the Russians are after.

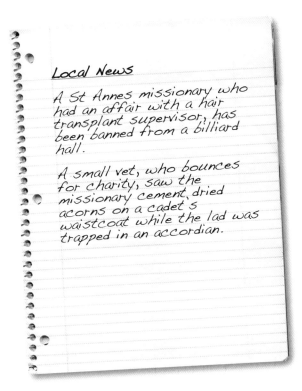

Local News

A St Annes missionary who had an affair with a hair transplant supervisor, has been banned from a billiard hall.

A small vet, who bounces for charity, saw the missionary cement, dried acorns on a cadet's waistcoat while the lad was trapped in an accordian.

Another body has been unearthed in the South Shore boarding house owned by Mrs Wretch, who is on trial for murdering holidaymakers that asked for more food. A private investigator, one Harold Plume, noticed that a frock hanging up in Mrs Wretch's wardrobe, seemed somewhat bulky. On closer scrutiny, Mr Plume was staggered to find inside the garment, pinned to the gusset, the corpse of an Arab pianist missing for nine weeks. When questioned in her cell, Mrs Wretch said angrily: "Oh 'im? Flamin' well walk about in a sheet all day, then asking for a dish of mutton and rice. I gave 'im rice alright, I bunged a tin of Ambrosia down 'is throat then got a cow to kick him." Rumour has it that Mrs.Wretch and Roscoe Chip, who is accused of blowing eggs through his vest, are getting very close in a romantic way.

___

A Warton ballcock moulder who shot a kite down with an onion left his wife a low light in a windmill.

___

A photograph of a parrot peeling a radish was stolen from a German athlete's biscuit tin that had been sunk in a Freckleton submarine pen. A reward is offered for the safe return of the photograph which really belongs to a nudist who used to do Hitler's eyebrows.

___

The Fleetwood clown who lost his trousers on a ferris wheel climbed down last night, stole a muffin and a horse blanket then climbed back up and sang There is Nothin' Like a Dame. His wife has run off with a chimney sweep who plays golf and his handicap is gas central heating.

___

In response to a letter that arrived yesterday, here is an extract from Swenska Veyonariska's novel, Trump:
"The dying hen lay dying, and it died, dying. Mario shook his head, shakily, as he shook it. Janine Du Pump sobbed and the sobs sobbing, sobbed."

"Singing in
the rain,
Les in
May 1986."

10 February 1983

The sale of turtle manure is to be stopped and that is official. My readers may recall that some time ago I mentioned that a Wolverhampton lay preacher with a bad arm fell in a parcel of the stuff and hair grew on his feet. Now reports are coming in that are quite alarming. A Mrs Bloomer in Gateshead, who went bald during the Blitz, bought some turtle manure, and after her husband had rubbed it well into her head, she started walking sideways like a crab, and then later on she tried to steam iron her ears. From Doncaster comes a story that a man who wanted a hairy chest to impress a spinster with money in the Post Office, smeared the manure over his torso and in the morning he found a bush growing in his belly button. Two days later, grass appeared under the bush and an hour later, a thatched cottage appeared under his armpit. Specialists think it could be a beauty spot.

The Frenchman who swallowed a bucket last week has been charged with swallowing a male nurse. A leading surgeon who saw a foot hanging from the Frenchman's mouth told me that in his opinion, "the bloody Frog's doing it on purpose." Personally, I've never liked the French, ever since the time my brother's window cleaner, who was a bell ringer, fell in the river Seine, and all the Parisians sang, "Ringing in the Seine".

"Christmas is a' coming and the geese are getting fat.
So please put a penny in the old man's hat.
If you haven't got a penny, a half penny will do.
If you haven't got a half penny... burn his cap."

That doggerel was written 37 years ago by Spencer Bugg who lost his wife in Burnley... she didn't die, he just lost her. Now, a woman who claims she is his wife ran him down on a lawn mower on the M1. Police are asking people to look out for a lady wearing a horse's head and carrying a blue lance. Mr Bugg said his wife had some odd ideas and used to throw pork up step ladders. "I don't want her back," he told me from inside the hole where he lives, and then we played Monopoly. Meanwhile, a worried plumber told a constable that a lawnmower chased him up a side road and a lance was hurled at his mini. When he mentioned that his attacker had a horse's head, he was breathalysed on the spot and his dog had its license endorsed.

Jo Jo Spittle and the Yarroo Punks are to play in concert at the Albert Hall. Their latest album, Throwing up in Gloves, is in the charts and should stay there. Jo Jo, who is 59 in six years' time, paints fish as a hobby.

A woman who claims she is the real Prince Philip said last night that she had been underdressed by a man from Venus. Our reporter, who doesn't do a lot, gave her a bun with a flag in it and she sang a sea shanty for him while he had a bath. Whoop's Tours have done it again! Next summer they are running coach trips through a Burmese swamp and for an extra £3 holidaymakers can sleep up a tree. The coach will leave Sandbach on Tuesday and with any luck, reach Rangoon the following year. Post-dated sandwiches will be provided and there will be a prize for the first person to put his leg through a pith helmet.

That great Northern movie maker, Harry Merrypepper, is to ask President Reagan to appear in pantomime in Catford with Shirley Temple's uncle. The Ugly Sisters will be played by two ugly sisters who write to Des O'Connor, and Buttons will be played by anybody with a freckled elbow.

Personals

In the name of pity, will Bendy Phillips the contortionist get in touch with his mother who wants the purse made from cow's a chin to be sent to her sister in Reading. Bendy's father is still sat on a bus with a bag of nuts and he's under starter's orders. This is the last time I will appeal to this idiot, and I will speak no more of Aunt Julie's frog stuck in the coffin. Susie says she'll let Arnold out when his mac comes back from the cleaners.

the **Dawson** *Slant*

17 February 1983

A pigmy Liberal who found explosive toffee in his trumpet is the latest victim of a hate campaign waged by a group, who want to see Cinderella banned as a pantomime. According to their spokesman, "Cinderella is the cry of the oppressed against the System, and can only lead to maltreatment of pumpkins and overtime for mice." Police suspect a crank is responsible, and are to interview the woman who claims she is the real Prince Philip. This lady who, over the years, has become a nuisance, stated that she could grow corn up her nose and during Lent she goes to a disco with the Pope.

"The trail winds ever on across the burning plain"…. an extract from Clay Cockle's diary. Cockle, first man to find the source of the M6, vanished last year whilst painting a caravan in burnt sienna. We have been given permission by his mistress, Abigail Frump, to sell his suspenders in order to raise money to send oysters to Uganda. Cockle, whose nephew had musical hair until his leg fell off, auctioned his knees for charity last April. A lot of people didn't like Cockle and I wasn't too happy myself, especially when he sandpapered our pet rhino in Crewe.

A horse which can read the Koran in Welsh was found stuck in a tub of pickled eggs last night. The horse, described by its owner as "an educated aid to rose-growing" suffered from shingles during the war, and once ate Churchill's hat.

A mugger who got mugged on his way from a mugging told me that crime is getting worse for criminals. "If things keep on the way they're going," he said dolefully. " I'd be a mug to go out mugging at night." Mr Justice Turnip, who firmly believes that innocent people are to blame for robberies, said in court: "When people get attacked, they shouldn't mention it. That way the crime wave wouldn't look as if it's going up and I would have more time to play Cluedo."

A little-known martial art comes to Blackpool next month. Nosi judo Kwai is an old form of defence perfected by a Nepalese monk who went deaf in Birmingham. In simple terms for the layman, it means 'training and nostrils to wrestle'. One expert, who has five dans on a wet handkerchief, will give an exhibition at the Floating Kidney Social Club, Marton Moss. Basically, there are five moves for attack (1) The screwed upper feint with left nostril to throw the opponent's chin; (2) Outer thrust sniffle and forward jab; (3) Side punch sneeze and half-nelson shove; (4) Flared counter flap lunge and mucus drop; and (5) Go home with a print.

Doctor Rhubarb's Corner

Question: Our pet walrus who died 15 years ago hasn't moved since. My husband plugged it in to the Christmas Tree and my son, who can't find his teeth, lost an apron. We never buried the walrus because our garden is on the roof and the woman next door is a Mormon. Could we exchange it for a Billy Daniels LP or perhaps stuff it with old shrimps whiskers?

Answer: A walrus is unpredictable when dead and its ears should be cemented up. Stand it on the edge of a damp wheel and rub it every day with glue. Laughter is a tonic, they say, and four teaspoons is enough. Put a scarf round the Mormon and never place warm eels in a bucket of scampi.

Readers' Jokes
This week, "Thin" jokes submitted by R. Suckett, of Swansea.
My wife is so thin she once fell through a string vest.
The wife is so thin we had to bend her double to get an X-ray picture.
My wife is so thin when the hairdresser's set on fire, she escaped through a roller.
Mr Suckett wins our star prize, a self-destruct shoe horn with a toffee bugle... well done.

Blackpool-based, Swiss-born scientist, Doctor Helmut Clack, told me that the smell of singed snow can often make a cat impotent.

"Les will be forever remembered for his Cissie and Ada partnership with Roy Barraclough."

Subscribers

Elizabeth Baker

Diana & Alan Bromley

Vaughan Cochrane

Jean Davies

Mrs Jean Davies

Alan Dove

Victoria Eaves

Geoffrey Fenton

Carol & Peter Ford

Pam & Alan Forrest

Jim Gibson

James Haselup

Tony Hughes

Ken Kitching

Kathleen Knott

Peter Lever

Norman Leyland

Kenny Logue

Mario (Little Ted)

Joan Mitton

Jacqueline Victoria Pratt

Francis Price

Ernie & Viv Sanderson

Sammy & Sylvia Sanderson

Mark Singleton

Alan Smith

Vera Todd

Vasudev Family

Andrew Walch

Steven West